Postcolonial Narrative
and the
Work of Mourning

SUNY series

———————————

EXPLORATIONS

in

POSTCOLONIAL STUDIES

———————————

Emmanuel C. Eze
and Arif Dirlik, editors

POSTCOLONIAL NARRATIVE
AND THE
WORK OF MOURNING

J. M. Coetzee, Wilson Harris, and Toni Morrison

SAM DURRANT

STATE UNIVERSITY OF NEW YORK PRESS

Published by
STATE UNIVERSITY OF NEW YORK PRESS, ALBANY

© 2004 State University of New York

For information, address State University of New York Press,
90 State Street, Suite 700, Albany, NY 12207

Production, Laurie Searl
Marketing, Michael Campochiaro

Library of Congress Cataloging-in-Publication Data

Durrant, Sam, 1970–
  Postcolonial narrative and the work of mourning : J. M. Coetzee, Wilson Harris, and Toni
Morrison / Sam Durrant.
     p. cm. — (SUNY series, explorations in postcolonial studies)
  Includes bibliographical references and index.
  ISBN 0-7914-5945-4 (alk. paper)
     1. Coetzee, J. M., 1940—Criticism and interpretation. 2. Morrison, Toni—Criticism and
interpretation. 3. Harris, Wilson—Criticism and interpretation. 4. African Americans in
literature. 5. South Africa—In literature. 6. Postcolonialism in literature. 7. Apartheid in
literature. 8. Guyana—In literature. 9. Slavery in literature. 10. Blacks in literature. 11.
Grief in literature. 12. Narration (Rhetoric) I. Title. II. Series.

PR9369.3.C58Z65 2003
813'.5409358—dc21
                                                                              2003045657

10   9   8   7   6   5   4   3   2   1

Contents

We know that the Jews were prohibited from investigating the future. The Torah and the prayers instructed them in remembrance however.

     —Walter Benjamin, "Theses on the Philosophy of History"

ACKNOWLEDGMENTS

This book began life as a Ph.D. Thesis at Queen's University, Ontario, and is particularly indebted to my supervisor, Asha Varadharajan, who taught a mind that is inclined to associate all too freely how to discriminate. Sylvia Söderlind, Jed Rasula, Neil Lazarus, Helen Tiffin, Rosemary Jolly, Carrie Dawson, and Derek Attridge all read drafts and provided generous commentary. Many thanks to the anonymous readers of the manuscript for their sympathetic and illuminating suggestions, to my colleagues, Stuart Murray and Shirley Chew at Leeds University, for vital guidance while revising the introduction, and to Jane Bunker, Laurie Searl, and the publishing team at SUNY Press. I am also profoundly grateful to Charles Shepherdson for his inspirational teaching; the graduate communities at University of Missouri-Columbia and Queen's University, especially Ella Ophir, Tom Kohut, and David Cuthbert; Susan Spearey and Annick Hillger, with whom I collaborated on conference panels; the Canadian Association for Commonwealth Literature and Language Studies, at whose conferences I presented early versions of some of the material; and the Ontario Graduate Scholarship Program for financial support. Most of all I would like to thank my mother and siblings for their constant love and support, and Alessandra Magri, to whom I am indebted for her meticulous editing of the final manuscript and for much, much more than I can say.

Material from chapter 1 was published as "Bearing Witness to Apartheid: J. M. Coetzee's Inconsolable Works of Mourning" in *Contemporary Literature* 40, 3 (1999): 430–63. Material from chapter 2 was published as "Hosting History: Wilson Harris's Sacramental Narratives" in *Jouvert: A Journal of Postcolonial Studies* 5, 1 (Autumn 2000) *http://social.chass.ncsu.edu/jouvert/v5i1/samdur.htm*.

SPECTERS OF COLONIALISM

He wants to put his story next to hers.

"Sethe," he says, "me and you got more yesterdays than anybody. We need some kind of tomorrow."

—Toni Morrison, *Beloved*

Without this non-contemporaneity with itself of the living present, without that which secretly unhinges it, without this respect for justice concerning those who are not there, of those who are no longer or who are not yet present and living, what sense would there be to ask the question "where?" "where tomorrow?" "whither?"

—Jacques Derrida, *Specters of Marx*

Postcolonial narrative, structured by a tension between the oppressive memory of the past and the liberatory promise of the future, is necessarily involved in a work of mourning. Its principal task is to engender a consciousness of the unjust foundations of the present and to open up the possibility of a just future, what Morrison's fugitive slave conceives of as "some kind of tomorrow" (*Beloved* 273). This book focuses on three contemporary writers whose work is exemplary in this regard: J. M. Coetzee, Wilson Harris, and Toni Morrison. Their novels invite us to participate in a ceaseless labor of remembrance, a labor which radically redefines the borders of community by teaching us how to live in memory of both the dead and all those whose living human presence continues to be disavowed by the present world order.

At the center of this study is a comparison of three modes of bearing witness to histories of racial oppression. Coetzee principally adddresses South

African apartheid, Harris the complex Caribbean history of genocide, slavery, and settlement, and Morrison, U.S. slavery and its legacies. While these histories are uneasily grouped together under the general heading of colonialism, the narratives that memorialize these histories are postcolonial in that they share a common horizon of emancipation, one that exceeds specific historical instances of liberation such as the U.S. Emancipation Proclamation in 1863, the independence of Guyana and other Caribbean nations in the 1960s and 1970s, and the multiracial elections in South Africa in 1994.[1] Although Morrison explicitly addresses her work, at least in the first instance, to an African American readership (Ruas 96), the work of all three writers is read throughout the English-speaking world and beyond, and forms part of a global conversation about the nature of contemporary community. Within the context of this international conversation, I retain the term "postcolonial" as a marker of the kind of cultural work I see each writer as carrying out. Their work is postcolonial in a performative sense: they bear witness to the various histories of racial oppression that underwrite local, national, and international privilege and continue to inform, if not determine, our cultural and psychological existence in the hope that their literary witnessing will bring into being a truly *post*colonial form of community.[2]

To understand our present as postcolonial is to raise the difficult question of the relation between postcolonialism and postmodernism (as schools of thought) and postcoloniality and postmodernity (as descriptions of our era). Certain postcolonial critics have attempted to distinguish between an apolitical or overly theoretical postmodernism that "marginalizes or rejects historical context" (Adam and Tiffin, cover notes) and a politically committed postcolonialism, grounded in the practicalities of political resistance. Such a distinction has been increasingly hard to maintain in the light of the ethico-political "turn" in those theorists loosely identified, despite their differences, as postmodern or poststructuralist. Derrida's *Specters of Marx,* for instance, from which I take my second epigraph, argues that deconstruction has always been fundamentally concerned with issues of justice, a claim complemented by Robert Young's argument that poststructuralism—and in particular deconstruction—arose historically out of the postwar crisis of the French empire and was always already, so to speak, postcolonial.

A related distinction between postmodernity as the (postpolitical) condition of Western states and postcoloniality as the (politicized) condition of newly independent states is similarly problematic. Postcolonial nations are necessarily subject to the neocolonial logic of late capitalism, and some form of "one world" theory is clearly necessary in order to think the possibility of "transnational social justice" (Young, *Postcolonialism* 427).[3] Although Young is quick to emphasize that there is no universal "'postcolonial condition' outside specific instances of complex interminglings of structural forces with local, personal experience" (*Postcolonialism* 57), postcolonialism—as a praxis—is nevertheless "grounded in an appeal to an ethical universal" entailing "a certain simple respect for human suffering" and a "fundamental revolt against [it]" (Appiah 353).[4]

My description of "our" era as postcolonial is thus an attempt to think global responsibility while paying attention to the differing degrees to which we are implicated in histories of oppression. Instead of pitting an irresponsible postmodernism against a responsible postcolonialism, I want to suggest that both movements are grounded in an awareness of historical injustice. While Young emphasises the significance of the Algerian war,[5] the more explicit and sustained reference in the work of Derrida and many of his contemporaries is the Holocaust, understood as a limit experience that radically alters our understanding of what it means to be human and makes it impossible to entertain notions of progress, culture, and even morality[6]—precisely the same Enlightenment beliefs that postcolonial theorists have argued colonialism calls into question, even at the historical moment in which these beliefs were being formulated. Postmodernism would thus appear to be haunted by the memory of the Holocaust in much the same way as postcolonialism is haunted by the memory of colonialism.

Aimé Césaire once argued that fascism was a form of colonialism brought home to Europe (Young, *Postcolonialism* 2). To link the two modes of racial oppression is not to challenge arguments concerning the uniqueness of the Holocaust nor to gloss over the differences between the extermination of the Jews and the many different forms of colonialism—few of which were genocidal in intention. What concerns me here is that both histories produce similar problems of memorialization. Although the historical time span of the two "events" is very different, the one taking place over roughly five hundred years and the other less than five,[7] the impact of both events exceeds the moment of their historical occurrence, acquiring the disturbed, belated chronology of trauma. While much work has been done on the difficulties involved in remembering the Holocaust, very little of this work has been drawn on in considerations of postcolonial literature. It is thus part of the intention of the present study to initiate a conversation between what have up to now remained the very distinct schools of postcolonial studies and Holocaust studies.

In so doing, I am following in the footsteps of Paul Gilroy, who makes the comparison explicit in his understanding of the Black Atlantic as a diasporic cultural formation constituted by the "sublime" memory of racial terror. Gilroy's use of the sublime is frustratingly undertheorized but seems to derive more from Edmund Burke's *A Philosophical Analysis into the Origin of Our Ideas of the Sublime and Beautiful* than from the Kantian tradition which informs the deconstructive and psychoanalytic understanding of the Holocaust. While

Burke analyzes the sublime primarily as a feeling or sensation, Kant explicitly places the sublime at the center of his theory of the subject, as a crucial part of the faculty of judgment that mediates between moral understanding and reason (Kant 5). The sublime induces a crisis of the subject (and thus a crisis in Kant's entire philosophical edifice) insofar as it temporarily overwhelms the subject's imaginative powers of presentation. According to Kant, the mind subsequently recovers itself by reproducing this incommensurability as an "idea of reason" and thereby discovering its "supersensible vocation."[8] Less convinced of the mind's ability to transcend experience, postmodern philosophers such as Jean-François Lyotard, to whom I shall return, understand the sublime as an irrevocable violence done to the imagination. It is as a breach or rupture in the subject's powers of presentation that the experience of the sublime is linked to the Freudian category of trauma. The "monstrous" histories of slavery, colonialism, or the Holocaust are sublime insofar as they do violence both to the individual and the collective imagination. Such events have been described as collective or cultural trauma not simply by aggregating the traumatic experiences of individual victims, but because they disrupt the "consciousness" of the entire community, destroying the possibility of a common frame of reference and calling into question our sense of being-in-common.

Toni Morrison, whom Gilroy quotes at length in his final chapter, shares this understanding of slavery as a crisis of subjectivity and community. The dedication of *Beloved* to "Sixty Million and more" who died during slavery and the Middle Passage has been read as a comparative reference to the six million victims of the Holocaust. However, her comparison is based not simply on questions of magnitude but on the impact of slavery in defining what it means to be modern.

> . . . modern life begins with slavery. . . . From a woman's point of view, in terms of confronting the problems of where the world is now, black women had to deal with post-modern problems in the nineteenth century and earlier. . . . These strategies for survival made the truly modern person. You can call it an ideology and an economy, what it is is a pathology. Slavery broke the world in half, it broke it in every way. It broke Europe. It made them into something else, it made them into slave masters, it made them crazy. You can't do that for hundreds of years and it not take its toll. They had to dehumanize, not just the slaves but themselves. They have had to reconstruct everything in order to make that system appear true. It made everything in world war two possible. It made world war one necessary. Racism is the word that we use to encompass all this. (Gilroy 221)

At the heart of histories of racism is the negation of the humanity of the other, an act of exclusion that has "pathological" consequences precisely because it introduces an internal exception into the category of the human.

In the United States, slavery is the excluded interior at the heart of its famous declaration that all men are created equal, an aporia that prevents both white and black Americans from constituting themselves as subjects. Morrison's words recall those of James Baldwin in his celebrated essay, "Stranger in a Village":

> It was impossible for Americans to accept the black man as one of themselves, for to do so was to jeopardize their status as white men. But not so to accept him was to deny his human reality, his human weight and complexity, and the strain of denying the overwhelmingly undeniable forced Americans into rationalizations so fantastic that they approached the pathological. (172)

Baldwin's argument is precisely worded: racism renders reason itself pathological. He argues that this pathology is uniquely American, in that European colonialism happened at a remove from Europe, which meant that the problem of the black man remained "comfortingly abstract" and thus "represented no threat to European identity" (170). While Baldwin's distinction may go some way to explaining the differences between European and American racism, a "history that happened elsewhere," as Homi Bhabha demonstrates in his reading of Salman Rushdie's *The Satanic Verses,* can prove no less pathological in its consequences.

Homi Bhabha invokes Freud's concept of *nachträglichkeit* or belatedness to describe the time lag that characterises the traumatic return of Britain's colonial history, personified in the figure of Gibreel Farishta in Salman Rushdie's *The Satanic Verses.* His analysis of the disjunctive temporality of (post)colonialism parallels Lyotard's analysis of how the Holocaust functions as a belated blow to European consciousness. The figure of the native, the black man or the Jew produces a crisis in European consciousness precisely because their existence as humans has to be denied in order for the European to retain a sense of his own subjectivity. Insofar as this denial founds the European subject, it constitutes the *prehistory* of the European subject. This denial is not a simple forgetting that occurred at a particular point in history (secondary repression) but a *foreclosure* of the very possibility of the other's humanity (primary repression).

Lyotard distinguishes between these two modes of forgetting by capitalizing the Forgetting involved in primary repression. While secondary repression constitutes a "representable, reversible forgetting," primary repression or foreclosure constitutes a "Forgetting that thwarts all representation" (5). He goes on to link secondary repression to Kant's aesthetic order, the realm of representation, and primary repression to the sublime, the order of the unrepresentable. What is unrepresentable or unnarratable about the Holocaust is not so much the details of the extermination camps but the Forgetting of Jewish humanity that allowed the Holocaust to take place in the first place. To recover a history of the Holocaust as an event that took place during the Nazi era is to ignore the fact that this Forgetting does not take place in historical time. Nor is it simply a matter of "explaining" the Holocaust by documenting the history of pogroms, discrimination, and internal and external exile that make up the history of European anti-Semitism. Such a history would still not be capable of remembering the Forgetting of Jewish humanity that is foundational to the construction of European identity. One can only trace the effects of this Forgetting; the fantastic existence of "the jews" as dirty, foreign, other, etc. hovers outside time as what Freud termed "unconscious affect"—formless, terrifying, unquantifiable.

Lyotard writes "the jews," in order to differentiate the ideological construction from actual Jews, a construction that nevertheless has real effects: "'The jews' are the object of a dismissal with which real Jews are afflicted in reality" (3). Narrative histories that seek to recover a Jewish or black subject must ignore the fact that the term "jew" or "black man" is in fact a racist construction, the figure of an exclusion. They chronologize "a time that is not chronological" (16) and thus function as a mode of insulation against the achronological, traumatic temporality of racism. "The decision to analyze, to write, to historize is made according to different stakes, to be sure, but it is taken, in each case, against this formless mass, and in order to lend it form, a place in space, a moment in temporal succession" (17). Postcolonial narrative is thus confronted with the impossible task of finding a mode of writing that would not immediately transform formlessness into form, a mode of writing that can bear witness to its own incapacity to recover a history.

Lyotard's suggestive analysis parallels that of Gayatri Chakravorty Spivak, who begins her monumental summing up of her vexed relation to postcolonial theory, mischievously entitled *A Critique of Postcolonial Reason*, by emphasising the centrality of the concept of foreclosure to her entire opus. The first chapter goes on to demonstrate how the putatively universal subject of the European Enlightenment is constituted by this primary act of exclusion. Major European philosophers such as Kant, Hegel, and Marx were unable to produce a concept of the human without simultaneously producing a *differend* (Lyotard's term), a radically incommensurable mode of being: Kant needs his New Hollander "creatures of less purposive form" (Spivak 33), Hegel his "Spirit-in-India" (44), and Marx his "Asiatic mode of production" (94) in order to elaborate their different narratives of human advancement. In later chapters, Spivak variously identifies this figure as the racial other, the subaltern or—in a bid to emphasize the continuities between the Enlightenment and seemingly more radical modes of *postcolonial* reason—the native informant.

Following Spivak's attempt to disaffiliate herself from the postcolonial enterprise, I was tempted to reorganize this book around the idea of the subaltern. However, rather than simply abandon the much criticized movement, I have sought to redefine it, contesting the mainstream understanding of postcolonialism as a recuperative, historicizing project and arguing for the centrality of a deconstructive, anti-historicist ethics of remembrance. In so doing, I hope to remain true to the spirit of Spivak's work, which, despite its attempt to position itself on the margins, has always self-reflexively operated as an exemplary *internal* critique of postcolonialism.

In linking the construction of the racial other to primary repression or foreclosure, Spivak, Lyotard, and Bhabha emphasize that it can never be a question of retrieving the other as a subject. Spivak's assertion that there is no "subaltern subject that can know and speak itself" ("Can the Subaltern Speak" 285) is in some ways simply a more severe version of Bhabha's traumatic return of the colonized: that which has been radically excluded from the category of the human is not presentable on the same plane of representation.

There are two responses to this exclusion: the first is what Bhabha dubs the "principle of avenging repetition." Flying high above London, Gibreel exclaims:

> Those powerless English! Did they not think that their history would return to haunt them? 'The native is an oppressed person whose permanent dream is to become the persecutor' (Fanon). . . . He would make this land anew. He was the Archangel Gibreel. And I'm back. (Rushdie 353, qtd. in Bhabha 169)

However Bhabha's celebration of Gibreel's attempt to "hybridize" London misses the way in which Gibreel's return is singularly untraumatic for its inhabitants, who simply experience a prolonged heatwave. As the quotation from Fanon suggests, it is Gibreel himself who remains truly haunted. His dreams of revenge remain just that—dreams—schizophrenic and self-destructive hallucinations that he can escape only by committing suicide.[9]

The alternative response is exemplified by that other angel, Benjamin's angel of history, who seeks not to avenge the dead but to remember them. It is the shadow of Benjamin's angel that lies behind Derrida's longing "for a justice that would finally be removed from the fatality of vengeance" (*Specters* 21). I shall return to Benjamin's angel in more depth in chapters 1 and 2, but for now suffice it to say that he haunts this book as *the* figure of inconsolable mourning, as the exemplary consciousness of the unjust foundation of the present. To "rename the postmodern from the perspective of the postcolonial" (Bhabha 175) is perhaps simply to recognize that colonialism, apartheid, slavery, and the Holocaust are, for all their historical differences, nevertheless part of the same "single catastrophe" to which the Angelus Novus bears witness ("Theses" 257–58).

Written in the spring of 1940, Benjamin's angel seems preternaturally aware of the Holocaust to come, even though, or rather *precisely because*, his gaze is fixed unwaveringly on the past. Benjamin concludes his essay with the words that form the epigraph to this book: "We know that the Jews were prohibited from investigating the future. The Torah and the prayers instructed them in remembrance however" (265). The angel's vigil is carried out in memory of the future. As Athos teaches the Holocaust survivor Jakob Beer, in Anne Michaels' *Fugitive Pieces*, "it is your future you are remembering" (21).[10] The possibility of a different future, a future that would not simply be a repetition of the past, is dependent on a never-ending labor of remembrance.

Postcolonialism is often explicitly conceived of as a memorializing project. Leela Gandhi argues that while newly independent states are often prone to a "will-to-forget" the past, postcolonialism (by which she principally means postcolonial theory) attempts to counter this amnesia by "revisiting, remembering and, crucially, interrogating the colonial past" (4). Her description of postcolonialism as a "therapeutic retrieval of the colonial past" (5) might initially seem to anticipate my conception of postcolonial narrative as a work of mourning. However, there are at least two important qualifications to be made here. First, one needs to investigate the kind of collective subject implied by the idea of postcolonialism as therapy. Second, the work of mourning is ultimately a recognition of the impossibility of retrieval—and it is this impossibility that renders the work of mourning interminable. Gandhi begins her book by acknowledging the inaugural status of Spivak's "Can the Subaltern Speak?" and ends by referring to the work of Lyotard, yet fails to recognize that their sustained critiques of the historicist fantasy of recovering or retrieving the past is radically at odds with her definition of postcolonialism.

The traumatic or achronological temporality of the postcolonial means that the term "postcolonial narrative" is always already at odds with itself, caught up in an impossible attempt to narrate a time that constantly eludes its telling. Nevertheless, my epigraph from *Beloved* would indicate that "some kind of tomorrow" is contingent on being able to transform a surplus of yesterdays if not into a conventional historical narrative, then at least into *some kind of* story. This basic impulse to narrate the past would suggest that postcolonial narrative seeks to perform some kind of therapy, even in the absence of retrieving a history. In this regard, the aim of postcolonial narrative would at first sight appear to be similar to that of psychoanalysis: "Analysis can have as its only aim the advent of authentic speech and the realization by the subject of its history in relation to a future" (Lacan, *Écrits* 302). However, the move from the individual case history to history itself, from a work of mourning that is centered on the recovery of the individual subject to a work of mourning that wishes to foster a sense of collective existence, entails a reappraisal of the ultimate purpose of mourning. For the individual, mourning would seem to be a process of learning how to bury the dead, how to attain what analysts refer to as "symbolic closure." For the collective, as Derrida argues, the possibility of a just future lies in our ability to live in remembrance of the victims of injustice, in our ability to conjure the dead rather than bury them. Psychoanalysis, with its commitment to the well-being of the subject, encourages us to exorcise our ghosts, to come to terms with loss and move on. Deconstruction, with its commitment to the other, to that which "unhinges" the subject, urges us to learn to live with ghosts. Postcolonial narrative, which addresses the individual reader both in his or her singularity and as a member of wider communities, is caught between these two commitments: its transformation of the past into a narrative is simultaneously an attempt to summon the dead and to lay them to rest.[11]

In chapter 1 I explore Derrida's notion of impossible or inconsolable mourning, which refuses the distinction between mourning and melancholia. However, the distinction is already problematic in Freud's original essay, "Mourning and Melancholia," which attempts to discriminate between a "healthy" process of remembering in order to forget and an "unhealthy" process of remembering that seems to have no end other than the perpetuation of the process of remembering itself. Freud categorizes the former process as mourning, the withdrawal of libido from the love object, the gradual acceptance of loss, and the latter as melancholia, the refusal to withdraw this affection, the denial of loss. However, even in the very attempt to establish a distinction between the two states, Freud is forced to admit that "with one exception, the same traits are met with in mourning" as in melancholia (244). Apart from what he describes as "a lowering of self-regarding feelings," it is only our sense of proportion, our sense of what constitutes a "reasonable" amount of time and emotional expenditure, that enables us to distinguish the one from the other. And this sense of what constitutes a healthy or reasonable period of mourning radically alters as we move toward the idea of collective mourning. At the level of the individual, the melancholic's refusal to recognize an end to the time of mourning seems to preclude the possibility of the future. For the collective, the commitment never to forget seems precisely to be a way of looking to the future, a way of ensuring that history does not repeat itself.[12]

The seemingly endless—both unceasing and purposeless—compulsion to repeat that characterizes both melancholia and the traumatic neuroses of the war victims that he had begun to treat produces a crisis in Freud's attempt to construct a theory of the instincts. "Mourning and Melancholia" (1917) is closely followed by such works as *Beyond the Pleasure Principle* (1920) and "The Economic Problem of Masochism" (1924). As a seemingly perverse or masochistic desire to repeat or linger over a painful experience, melancholia seems to contradict not only the pleasure principle but also the life-instinct, the seemingly incontrovertible thesis that all organisms desire to live. Melancholia is for Freud inexplicable evidence of a being-for-death, even of a will to die. A state, therefore, to be strongly discouraged. And yet the psychoanalytic session seeks to promote a process of repetition that is only to be distinguished from melancholia by its overall intention. This is the psychoanalyst's gambit: to distinguish between "involuntary" repetition and an active process of working through, between melancholia and mourning. And not merely to distinguish the one from the other but also to transform the one into the other by assigning the process of repetition an end—a purpose, direction, and finitude. The psychoanalytic session thus attempts both to initiate and to limit the work of mourning. Like the cathartic rituals of Greek tragedy, it allows the display of disproportionate or immoderate grief within the constraints of a "safe," formal setting.

In *Mrs Dalloway,* a novel contemporaneous with Freud's attempts to deal with the enigma of the repetition compulsion, Virginia Woolf rages against a Harley Street doctor who sees the traumatic neurosis of a shell-shocked soldier as evidence of a lack of "a sense of proportion" (96).[13] Woolf goes on to link the doctor's desire for proportion to the intolerance of otherness at the heart of Britain's attempt to colonize the world (100). But there is a fine line between the doctor's sense of proportion, which refuses the perspective of the mad, and Mrs Dalloway's own sense of aesthetic order, which attempts to accommodate the soldier's decision to die within her own celebration of life, to acknowledge the presence of death even as it appears in "the middle of [her] party" (183). The challenge for both Freud and Woolf is to provide a space in which one might do justice to the sense of disproportion engendered by the traumatic experience of war, to construct, as it were, a "home" for disproportion. A similar challenge is faced by the postcolonial novelist. One of the central tasks of this study will be to determine the degree to which each novelist's attempt to house the sense of "disproportion" engendered by racial oppression constitutes an attempt to assign a limit to the work of mourning. Should postcolonial novelists follow the example of psychoanalysis and seek to transform melancholia into mourning, or should they allow the endlessness of grief to overwhelm the literary work? Should their work offer some form of healing or closure or continue to testify to the disproportionate memories of racial oppression by somehow transgressing the limits of their own composition?

The literary analysis that makes up the bulk of this study might thus be described as the attempt to determine the significance of particular acts of repetition. Various characters perform rituals that one might be tempted to describe as pathological instances of a repetition compulsion. However, insofar as these characters are not simply mimetic representations of individual subjects, their grief cannot simply be regarded as a private affair. Part of my task will be to show how their melancholic rituals accrue a wider political significance and thus need to be reinterpreted as modes of collective mourning. To put it another way, their immoderate grief needs to be recognized as a precisely proportionate response to history, a way of bearing witness to losses that exceed the proportions of the individual subject.[14]

On the meta-textual level, all three of the writers that I have chosen to study are themselves engaged—however obliquely—in a repetition of history. If we emphasize the writer's experience of feeling compelled to write, then perhaps we should characterize writing itself as a mode of repetition compulsion. Certainly, all three writers could be accused of writing the same novel over and over again, as if each repetition were insufficient to lay the past to rest, or even as if the writer were gaining a masochistic pleasure from returning to the same violent scenes of racial oppression. But if we conceive of writing as a more or less voluntary or deliberate activity, then postcolonial narrative presents itself as a mode of mourning, as a way of consciously working through history. The possibility—indeed the inevitability—that the writer is working through his or her own personal history falls outside the concerns of this study. While novels such as Coetzee's *Age of Iron*, written directly after the loss of three family members, are clearly ways of working through personal losses, my focus on collective mourning is deliberately anti-autobiographical.[15] I want to examine the possibility that a writer performs an exemplary act of working through history itself, and that, in reading his or her work, we too become involved in this process of working through history.

This process is not quite collective or communal in the usual sense of the term. Unlike a religious ceremony or a tragic drama, the novel is a private experience that makes a singular appeal to each of its readers, even as it evokes the idea of some sort of community of readers. And this singularity of appeal is perhaps its peculiar merit, for it allows a certain mediation between the personal and the collective, the ethical and the political. It is tempting to argue that the novel allows the reader to experience the political as the personal, to work through collective loss as if it were his or her own. But it is equally possible to argue that the novel forces the reader to confront his or her insertion in the collective, the way in which one's own history, as Cathy Caruth puts it, "is never simply one's own" (192). Thus it might be more accurate to say that postcolonial narrative enables us to work through our *relation* to history; it is not a communal act so much as an act of creating community.

The idea of relation has been the lifelong preoccupation of the Caribbean philosopher and writer, Edouard Glissant. In his most recent collection, entitled *Poetics of Relation*, Glissant seeks to establish the basis for a new cross-cultural humanism. In the opening essay, "The Open Boat," Glissant speaks of the Middle Passage from Africa to the New World as an "abyss" that marks the difference of Caribbean cultural community. However, though this experience made you, original victim of the sea's abysses, an exception, it became something shared and made us, the descendants, one people among others. People do not live on exception. Relation is not made up of things that are foreign but of shared knowledge. This experience of the abyss can now be said to be the best element of exchange. (8)

Echoing Caruth, Glissant concludes with an assertion of the potential exemplarity—even commonality—of the Caribbean experience as what one might describe as an anti-foundational foundation for cross-cultural community: "Our boats are open and we sail them for everyone" (9).

Postcolonial communities are in one sense as variously constituted as the colonial histories to which they seek to relate. They may be founded not on an openness toward others but rather on local, national, or racial exclusivity: forms of so-called strategic essentialism built around an oppositional sense of identity or sameness. Nevertheless, as the term "strategic" suggests, these formulations of community are responses to specific historical circumstances: the negritude movement of the 1920s, 1930s, and 1940s was a response to the racism of colonial rule and part of the wave of anticolonial cultural nationalism that led to the breakup of empire in subsequent decades. Although many movements have had recourse to essentialist models of identity in the postcolonial era, the long-term goal invariably remains the formation of a new, truly inclusive sense of community, what Leela Gandhi refers to as "the postnational promise of a genuine cosmopolitanism" (136).

However, this genuine cosmopolitanism or new humanism is not simply a return to the values of the Enlightenment. Rather, it seeks to contest the seemingly inclusive but actually exclusive sense of community inaugurated by philosophers such as Immanuel Kant. Spivak's critique of Kant parallels Foucault's response to Kant's "What is Enlightenment?" Kantian universalism is in fact a tacit imposition of a particular concept of what it means to be human on the rest of humanity.

> Foucault establishes that the Kantian concept of mankind is prescriptive rather than descriptive. Instead of reflecting the radical heterogeneity of human nature, it restricts the ostensibly universal structures of human existence to the normative condition of adult rationality—itself a value arising from the specific historicity of European societies. It follows that this account of "humanity" precludes the possibility of dialogue with other ways of being human and in fact brings into existence and circulation the notion of the "non-adult" or "inhuman." (Gandhi 32)

The challenge here is that for a community to remain open to the "radical heterogeneity of human experience" it would not be able to assume a common understanding of what it means to be human, would not even be able to reach consensus on what constitutes human rights. Is it possible to found a community on a recognition of our infinite difference? Such a question cannot be answered in this study, and indeed remains important precisely as a question that cannot be answered, as a question that perpetually disrupts the will to power inherent in any attempt to define the human. Insofar as postcolonial narrative is all too aware of the consequences of this will to power, one of its tasks is precisely to keep open the question of what constitutes the human.[16]

The idea of narrative as a form of communal address takes on a particular resonance for the writer who attempts to bear witness to histories of exclusion. Here the act of writing becomes simultaneously a way of protesting a failure of community and an attempt to bring into being a new form of community. This double motivation is at the heart of Toni Morrison's conception of her art as "the fully realized presence of a haunting" ("Honey and Rue Program Notes," qtd. in Bhabha 12), which Homi Bhabha translates into a "statement on the political responsibility of the critic, [who] must attempt to fully realize, and take responsibility for, the unspoken, unrepresented pasts that haunt the historical present" (12). Such a commitment echoes Derrida's respect for those who are "not there . . . those who are no longer or who are not yet present and living" (*Specters of Marx* xix). It challenges Marx's injunction in "The Eighteenth Brumaire" to let the dead bury the dead (597) and recalls not only Walter Benjamin's warning that "even the dead will not be safe if the enemy wins" ("Theses" 255) but also the emphasis in many non-Western cultures, such as that of the Yoruba, on the bonds that tie the living both to the dead and to the unborn.[17]

However, Bhabha's "translation" of Morrison's suggestive phrase glosses over two important problems. First, what is the specific nature of this act of "realization"? Bhabha is keen to avoid the word *representation,* for he recognizes that it is not simply a matter of representing the unrepresented, but of bearing witness to the way in which the "unrepresented pasts" haunt the present. Bhabha himself cites two postcolonial narratives that attempt to "house" the racial memories that haunt the present: Nadine Gordimer's *My Son's Story* and Morrison's *Beloved.* Unfortunately, as I argue in chapter 3, his all too cursory analysis of *Beloved* leads to a serious misreading of Morrison's novel. The political, ethical, and aesthetic complexity of bearing witness demands the kind of sustained textual analysis for which Bhabha never seems to have time.

Second, Bhabha fails to consider the specific relation of the individual writer to these "unrepresented pasts." To borrow Foucault's famous query, "What difference does it make who is speaking" ("What Is an Author?" 120)? What does it mean for a white writer such as Nadine Gordimer to "take responsibility for" South Africa's "unrepresented pasts?" Is her political and ethical responsibility the same as Morrison's? I have deliberately chosen to look at narratives by writers of different racial affiliations in order to show how the degree to which postcolonial writers are implicated in histories of racial oppression determines the nature of their literary witness and the ethico-political significance of their work of mourning.

Writers of, respectively, white South African, mixed Guyanese, and African American descent, Coetzee, Harris, and Morrison incorporate spectral presences into their narratives as a way of bearing witness to histories of exclusion. To open one's art to the fully realized presence of a haunting is to practice what one might call a postcolonial ethics—and aesthetics—of hospitality, to "leave an empty place, always, in memory of the hope—this is the very place of spectrality" (Derrida, *Specters* 65). Instead of seeking, like Orpheus, to wrench the other into the light of day, to render her fully present, they teach us how to remember the other's irretrievable difference.[18]

However, the radical heterogeneity of the other—Derrida translates Levinas' axiom *"tout autre est tout autre"* as "everyone is completely other" (*The Gift of Death* 68)—needs to be distinguished from the material history of othering, the violent negation or foreclosure of subjectivity that characterises the history of racism. Frantz Fanon famously dramatizes this experience of negation in a semiautobiographical chapter of *Black Skin, White Masks* entitled "The Fact of Blackness": "In the white world the man of colour encounters difficulties in the development of his bodily schema. Consciousness of the body is solely a negating activity" (110). The semiautobiographical way in which Fanon uses the pronoun "I" is designed to assert the commonality of his experience, to show how racism necessarily blurs the distinction between individual and collective trauma. The first line of the chapter: "Dirty Nigger! Or simply, "Look, a Negro!" (109) interpolates Fanon not as an individual but as a member of a race, a race understood not as one human race among others, but as something apart, other, nonhuman.[19] The experiences of racism that he goes on to recount do not add up to a narrative precisely because they cannot be integrated into a life history; they are repetitions of an "originary" event that bars him from having a life history and from the temporality of the human. This is dramatized in the syntax of Fanon's prose: he ends one paragraph with "And then . . ." (original ellipsis) and begins the next "And then the occasion arose when I had to meet the burden of the white man's eyes" (110). The repetition of temporal markers is bitterly ironic, for the encounter with the white man's eyes does not take at a specific moment in time, but repeats itself throughout a chapter of false starts and denied entries, encounters that never become meetings, never *lead* to anything except another encounter. "Battered down by tom-toms, cannibalism, intellectual deficiency, fetishism, racial defects, slave ships and, above all else, above all: 'Sho' good eatin'" (112), the narrative "I" is forced to give up its project of becoming a "man among other men" (112) and instead retreats into the collective negation assigned to it and attempts to make this uninhabitable zone habitable: for this is precisely the project of the negritude writers to whom Fanon "then" turns.

However, the words of Léopold Senghor and Aimé Césaire cannot restore that which was lost in the encounter with the white man, a loss that has already turned the whole chapter into a work of mourning: "On that day, completely dislocated, unable to be abroad with the other, the white man . . . I took myself off from my own presence, far indeed, and made myself an object. What else could it be but a hemorrhage that spattered my whole body with black blood" (112). By the time this body is given back to him, it appears "sprawled out, distorted, recolored, clad in mourning in that white winter day" (113). Fanon's hyperreal images suggest that the "fact" of blackness is not the natural or original color of his skin but something with which his body is first "splattered" and then "clad." Blackness becomes a way of remembering the forced departure of the self from its own habitation.

Crucially, blackness becomes both the sign of an originary violence done to the body (the black blood that spatters his body) *and* the memorialization of that violation (the mourning clothes with which his body is clad). Because blackness is thus instantiated both as wound and as memory of the wound there can be no forgetting, no end to the mourning. Unlike mourning clothes, human skin cannot be relinquished after a certain period and the attempts of the negritude poets to affirm blackness as a positive term ultimately prove ineffectual—they cannot, it seems, make the black body habitable, for the narrative "I" ends the chapter in limbo, lost in an inconsolable mourning: "Without responsibility, straddling Nothingness and Infinity, I began to weep" (140).

In *Fanon's Dialectic of Experience*, Ato Sekyi-Otu convincingly demonstrates that a "dramatic narrative structure" is in play throughout Fanon's work. "The Fact of Blackness" particularly demands to be read in a "literary" fashion not simply because it turns to poetry nor even because it dramatizes the problem of making a narrative out of an experience that does not take place in historical time, but because it has exemplary recourse to an *image* of the violated body in order to turn itself into a work of mourning. In a lecture entitled "By Force of Mourning" on the recently deceased Louis Marin and his "great book" *Pouvoirs de L'Image*, Derrida argues, and it is impossible to do justice to the "force" of his argument, that the image is always already involved in a work of mourning because it is an attempt to make the presence of an absence, of something other than itself, felt. The image is not simply "the weakened reproduction of what it would imitate," as in the Platonic tradition of *mimesis*, but has its own force precisely because it resists the logic of ontology or being: although it is not present in itself, it nevertheless exerts a certain power to move (177). And the image comes into its own, so to speak, when representing not simply an absence, but death itself:

It is in the re-presentation of the dead that the power of the image is
exemplary. . . . Representation here is no longer a simple reproductive
representation; it is such a recrudescence or resurgence of presence
thereby intensified, that it gives to be thought the lack, the default of
presence or the mourning that had hollowed out in advance the so-called
primitive or originary presence, the so-called living presence. (178)

In more familiar terms, the image operates as a supplement that makes us feel
a lack in the original; the dead are somehow more present to us in the image
than they were in real life.

This excessive power of the image to re-present, in the temporal lag that
Derrida refers to as "the time of reading" (189), something to us that was not
immediately apparent or accessible brings us closer to understanding the
peculiar force with which Fanon's body returns both to himself and to his
readers on that white winter's day. It returns from "the other side," offering
itself as an image of a death that occurs, invisibly, every time the white gaze
confronts the black body. It returns to us as an image, to borrow the title of
Elaine Scarry's profound meditation, of the body in pain, as the sign of a pain
that otherwise remains impossible to communicate: "what else could it be for
me but an amputation, an excision, a hemorrhage that spattered my whole
body with black blood" (112). The image searches for its own expression,
refusing the imitative structure of simile ("it felt *like* an amputation") to assert
the materiality or literality of an experience that was excessively real in its
impact, a blow that has irrevocably altered its recipient's relation to reality.
Ironically invoking the Freudian-Lacanian model of development to describe
an encounter that places the black man outside the time of the subject, Fanon
comments: "In the white world the man of color encounters difficulties in the
development of his bodily schema" (111).

Fanon's image of the body in pain thus functions to indicate a breach
in time; it memorializes a traumatic event without placing it within a
chronology. It does not retrieve an encounter with the white man's gaze
that occurred at a particular place and time but rather marks an experience
that is unhistoricizable both because it repeats itself infinitely, in Fanon's
life and in the lives of other black men (and, in a different form, the lives
of black women), and because the experience is in and of itself an experience of the breakdown of chronology, a confirmation that the black man is
indeed, to paraphrase Hegel, outside history, forcibly excluded from the
time of modernity.

The same logic is evident in Gayatri Chakravorty Spivak's presentation
of the female subaltern as that which cannot be represented *except by means of
an image,* or more precisely by an image of death, one that "marks the place of
her disappearance" ("Can the Subaltern Speak" 306). Spivak shows how the
agency of the female or "sexed" subaltern is circumscribed on the one hand by

British imperialism and on the other by patriarchal Indian nationalism. She then ends her essay by recounting the fate of Bhuvaneswari Bhaduri. In 1926, unable to carry out a political assassination on behalf of an anti-imperialist group, Bhuvaneswari waited until she was menstruating before hanging herself in order to make it clear that she had not committed suicide to avoid the shame of an illegitimate pregnancy. After all the dense and painstaking theorizing, Spivak leaves us with the sublime or monstrous image of a menstruating corpse as a bodily testament to the "no place from which the sexed subaltern can speak" (307).

Like Fanon's own hemorrhaging body, Bhaduri's corpse is an excessively "graphic" representation of the material effect of otherwise invisible forces. As in "The Fact of Blackness," the image of death arises in the place where a narrative history or life story ought to begin. Crucially for a study of postcolonial narrative, this pattern repeats itself in Spivak's translations of Mahasweta Devi's short stories. "Draupadi" ends with the image of the violated body of a tortured female freedom fighter, while "The Breast-Giver" ends with the erupting cancerous breasts of a woman forced to capitalize on their "magical" productivity to feed her family (*In Other Worlds* 179–209). These images also "speak" of the no-place from which the sexed subaltern can speak; the women acquire a degree of agency only by revealing the extent of their objectification. Operating as what Spivak describes "terrifying super-object[s]" (184), their bodies acquire, at the moment of death, the force of images that burn themselves into our memory. They bear sublime witness to the "originary" Forgetting of the sexed subaltern subject.

Although Spivak's attention to gender exposes an aporia in Fanon's thinking of race, both writers draw attention to the simultaneously invisibility and supervisibility of the racially marked body. On the one hand, the institutional racist gaze quite simply refuses to see the racially marked. As Coetzee notes "the response of South African legislators to [black suffering] is simply to keep it out of sight," to disavow—by force of law—the presence of the black labor force that inhabits the townships on the outskirts of the cities (*Doubling the Point* 361). The doctrine of *terra nullius,* one of the central ideological features of European colonization, amounts to a similar foreclosure of the possibility of native presence, an all too literal evacuation of the landscape. And I have already noted the Forgetting of the black subject at the heart of the US Declaration of Independence. On the other, the racially marked "subject" haunts the white imagination as a spectre that is all too visible, as if the denial of the racially marked's subjectivity causes the other to return as an irresistible body, as an all too physical threat or temptation.[20]

This double movement determines the curious *materiality* of the specters that haunt postcolonial narrative. As a way of bearing witness to the negation of subjectivity at the heart of apartheid, Coetzee incorporates foreign bodies into his narratives, bodies that remain obdurately unfamiliar despite the close attentions of his narrators. Wilson Harris structures each of the novellas that make up *The Guyana Quartet* around the incarnation or transubstantiation of what Wilson Harris refers to as the "absent body" of the civilizations that were eclipsed by the colonization of the Americas. And Toni Morrison's *Beloved* attempts to recall the "disremembered" victims of the Middle Passage by staging the corporeal return of the murdered daughter of an ex-slave. However, all three writers bear witness to the denial of subjectivity at the heart of racial oppression by denying their specters the status of fully realized characters. These specters remain unhomely or uncanny subjects precisely because the narratives are unable to render them familiar by retrieving their respective histories. As in Fanon's failed attempt to produce a narrative of racism, such figures cannot be plotted according to the time and space of the subject.

As a white South African, Coetzee's relation to black South Africans—or rather to the apartheid construction of "the blacks"—is perhaps closest to Lyotard's conception of the relationship of "European consciousness" to "the jews." As Coetzee laments in his 1987 Jerusalem Prize Acceptance Speech, "you cannot resign from the [master] caste. You can imagine resigning, you can perform a symbolic act of resignation, but short of shaking the dust of the country off your feet, there is no way of actually doing it" (*Doubling the Point* 96). This awareness of his own implication in the oppression of black South Africa opens up an irreducible gap in his narratives between the privileged position of his narrators and the oppressed position of the figures of alterity whose lives the narrators so desperately want to relate. Rather than attempting to recover the subjectivity of black South Africans, his novels bear witness to the act of Forgetting that underpins apartheid. The materiality or objectivity of his figures of alterity is a function of his inability to relate to them as subjects, his inability to transcend the "stunted" relations of apartheid. They stand in for a base level of suffering that resists narrativization not simply because the suffering is in itself unspeakable, but because his awareness of his own position of privilege prevents him from speaking on behalf of their suffering. In this sense, Coetzee's narratives are unable to work through the history of apartheid; they bear witness to a history of suffering that they are powerless to lay to rest.

Harris's mixed racial inheritance, the general confusion of color lines that characterises Guyanese and Caribbean society, and the distance generated by his position as a writer in (voluntary) exile in the UK, lead him to adopt a much more cross-cultural sense of his own implication in history. For Harris, it is the present in general—modernity, contemporary civilization—that has forgotten the history of colonization on which it is founded. Rather than speaking from the perspective of the oppressor or the oppressed, Harris sees himself as the shamanic medium through whom the dead come to express themselves in the lives of the living. Whereas Coetzee's narrators are unable to reduce the gap between themselves and the world of suffering, Harris's narrators take this suffering upon themselves. For Harris, to bear witness is to bridge the divide between subject and object, activity and passivity. This understanding of bearing witness as an act of mediation transforms suffering into a mode of redemption: the materiality of his spectral presences is precisely what *enables*, rather than disables, the work of mourning.

Like Coetzee, Morrison is forced to define the perspective from which she speaks in racial terms. In her fiction, scholarly work, and interviews, Morrison unambiguously assumes the burden of speaking on behalf of her race. However, her position is not without its own problems of articulation and remembrance. If Coetzee's narratives confront the problem of how to relate a history from which one remains irrevocably distanced, Morrison's narratives confront the problem of how to relate a history that remains too close, too proximate. The traumatic memory of slavery and the Middle Passage opens up something resembling an internal *differend* within Morrison's work, one that marks the gap between the subjective act of narration and the traumatic experience of racial oppression in which one is the object rather than the subject of one's history. Like Coetzee's work, her novels end up bearing witness to what she calls the "unbeing" of the racially marked "subject," but from the perspective of one who is herself racially marked. For Morrison, as for Coetzee, the materiality of the specter is the sign of a failure of mourning, an inability to verbalize a history of oppression. While Harris's narratives perform an act of spectral—indeed spiritual—homecoming, Morrison's specter, like Coetzee's figures of alterity, ultimately remains unhoused by the narrative in which she appears; the narrative is unable to accommodate the disproportionate dimensions of Beloved's racial memory, who ultimately has to be exorcised into the novel's epilogue. Nevertheless, while the narrative is unable to reclaim the disremembered, Beloved's presence does enable those to whom she returns to come to terms with their own personal histories. In this respect Morrison's work lies midway between that of Coetzee and Harris, remaining inconsolable on one level while offering a degree of consolation and healing on another.

For Coetzee, writing is clearly a response to what he describes as his feelings of helplessness before the fact of suffering in the world. His novels seem to replay the agony of his implication in apartheid. In this sense, then, his novels would seem to be manifestations of a melancholic or even masochistic repetition compulsion. At the same time, however, they are a mode of protesting this forced affiliation. They are thus minimal, highly qualified forms of action; as a mode of waiting for the end of apartheid, they too hover undecidably between activity and passivity. If they are less redemptive than Harris's narratives, it is because it is ethically impossible for Coetzee to absolve himself of the crimes of apartheid. If his fiction invites the title of postmodern allegory, this is less because he engages in metatextual "playfulness" than because his own agonistic relation to apartheid parallels that of European writers to the Holocaust. I thus relate his determination to remain inconsolable to the secular post-Holocaust tradition that informs both deconstruction and negative dialectics.

Harris's narratives, by contrast, enact an affirmative or "gay" mode of mourning in which consciousness of one's responsibility for history is transfigured into the lightest of burdens. Mindful of the catastrophes of history, Harris argues that art needs to offer a way out of the nihilism of historical determinism, an understanding of the repetitive nature of history that does not engender a fatalistic sense of despair. I thus relate Harris's "infinite rehearsal" to Friedrich Nietzsche's thought of eternal return, which eschews a static conception of history in favor of an affirmation of the constant "becoming" of existence. While Coetzee's art constitutes a Beckettian mode of waiting *for* redemption, Harris's art conceives of itself *as* an act of redemption, as an active intervention or transfiguration of history. Harris's understanding of bearing witness refuses the distinction between passive witnessing and active participation in the world, turning his art into a passionate activity in which the artist takes on the world's suffering and endows it with redemptive significance. For Harris, the idea of redemption is not teleological because existence has no end point: the rehearsal is infinite, the world is in a perpetual state of becoming. Thus while Harris's view of art as transformation is radically different from Coetzee's conception of art as a vigil, for both writers there can be no end to the work of mourning.

The novels of Coetzee and Harris might be described as modes not only of mourning but also of expiation, even if the possibility of absolution is necessarily deferred in Coetzee's work. In that they confront the phenomenon of "survivor's guilt," Morrison's novels might also be described as a mode of expiation. The structure of *Beloved* suggests that "some kind of tomorrow" for those who survived slavery is predicated on negotiating the claims of those who did not. The significance of Morrison's narratives as acts of repetition hinges on the difference between claiming and being claimed by one's history. On the one hand, her novels are an attempt to reclaim an African American sense of identity and history. Insofar as *Beloved* is able to memorialize the "Sixty Million and more" that died during the Middle Passage and slavery, it functions as a mode of what I term cultural memory. Cultural memory constitutes a healthy mode of mourning, which has as its aim the recovery of an African American subject. However, to the extent that the novel is unable to retrieve these anonymous victims from their historical limbo, unable to meet their infinite demand for remembrance, the novel succumbs to the melancholia of what I identify as racial memory, a collective memory of negation that threatens to overwhelm the individual with the consciousness of a "disproportionate" loss.

Morrison's approach to mourning is more redemptive than that of Coetzee and less consolatory than that of Harris, insistent on the necessity both of remaining inconsolable and of gaining a degree of closure. It is thus perhaps appropriate that my third chapter draws most heavily on psychoanalysis, that "secular religion" perpetually in crisis over whether it is able to call an end to the work of mourning and pronounce the patient cured. My use of psychoanalysis takes the risk of deploying a Eurocentric vocabulary to analyze a text and a culture that is only partly indebted to European modes of thought. If, as Morrison argues, slavery is central to the narrative of modernity, then it could be argued that psychoanalysis, understood as a response to the experience of modernity, is not so far removed from the experience of African Americans, that the African American is in fact an exemplary modern subject. Nevertheless, it remains crucial not to assume the a priori truth of the psychoanalytic account. Chapter 3 thus seeks only to place Morrison's story "next to" the Freudian/Lacanian account, rather than reading the novel in the light of the truth of the theory. To juxtapose their stories is to respect their integrity as different yet analogous modes of cultural thought. My model here is Frantz Fanon's own vexed relationship to psychoanalysis, a relation that Ato Sekyi-Otu has persuasively demonstrated is also analogical:

> Fanon ultimately gives psychoanalytic language no more and no less than an analogic or metaphoric function, as distinct from a foundational or etiological one, in accounting for the condition of the colonized and their dreams. . . . To the Lacanian dictum that "the unconscious is structured like a language," Fanon might have responded that the dreams of the colonized may well be structured like the language of neurosis but that they are occasioned by the language of political experience. (8)

Of course, Fanon's writing follows in the spirit of Freud's own writing, which, despite its intermittent desire to present psychoanalysis as an empirical science, has recourse to scientific knowledge frequently only by way of analogy; even his celebrated "topography" of the human mind is ultimately no more, or less, than an extended metaphor.

What follows, then, is an attempt to articulate a postcolonial ethics of remembrance. I hope to show that this ethics of remembrance determines both the formal structure—what Peter Brooks would call the desire—of the postcolonial narrative and the nature of each writer's engagement with the political. My readings are not intended to be comprehensive accounts of each writer's *oeuvre*, although they do attempt to effect a shift in the reception of

each writer's work. They are instead intended to exemplify a critical approach
that might bring us closer to an understanding of how postcolonial literature—and indeed literature in general—functions as collective memory, or
rather how literature strives to engage us *as* a collective, how it invites us to
participate in the *creation* of community.

CHAPTER ONE

SPEECHLESS BEFORE APARTHEID

J. M. Coetzee's Inconsolable Works of Mourning

> One of the souls was weeping. "Do not suppose, mortal" said this
> soul addressing him, "that because I am not substantial these tears
> you behold are not the tears of a true grief."
>
> —J. M. Coetzee, *Foe*

The South African Truth and Reconciliation Commission (TRC), in line
with the basic Freudian insight that we are destined to repeat that which we
fail to work through, was set up "to establish the truth in relation to past
events as well as the motives for and circumstances in which gross violations
of human rights occurred, and to make the findings known in order to prevent a repetition of such acts in future" (Preamble to the "Promotion of
National Unity and Reconciliation Act, 1995" qtd. in Dawes, para. 9).[1] But
how does one create the collective subject that a national process of working
through would seem to presume in a country where racial groups are so very
differently implicated in their country's history? What kinds of truth, what
modes of working through, bring about reconciliation? What is the relationship between the testimony of apartheid's victims and the confessions of
apartheid's perpetrators and between both these forms of truth telling and
the recovery of factual truth? Is reconciliation simply dependent on "estab-
lishing the [factual] truth in relation to past events" or does it require some
demonstration of grief on the part of victims and perpetrators alike? What
happens when a surfeit of factual truth is offered, as in the amnesty appeal of

the *Vlakplaas* officer Dirk Coetzee, almost as a substitute for an authentic admission of remorse?[2] What happens when truth is reduced to information?

As a way of indicating the enormity of the task before the Commission, a sceptical prospective commissioner suggested that "only literature can perform this miracle of reconciliation" (Krog 18). Without wishing either to dismiss the effectiveness of the TRC or to romanticize the role of literature, I want to interrogate the idea that literature can offer a way of working through a collective history by examining three of Coetzee's earlier novels. Written during the 1980s, at the height of the apartheid era, these novels testify to the suffering engendered by apartheid precisely by refusing to translate that suffering into a historical narrative. Rather than providing a direct relation of the history of apartheid, Coetzee's narratives instead provide a way of relating *to* such a history. They teach us that the true work of the novel consists not in the factual recovery *of* history, nor yet in the psychological recovery *from* history, but rather in the insistence on remaining inconsolable *before* history.

The truth-telling aspect of Coetzee's narratives consists not in the presentation of factual information but in the attempt to demonstrate a "true grief," a grief that acquires a certain materiality or historical weight despite the insubstantial, fictional context. In "The Inferno," the shade's tears call forth a reciprocal response from Dante, who, like the reader, is moved by the suffering of the damned. Dante's tears bear transgressive witness to the tyranny of God's Law,[3] but they cannot effect reconciliation because Dante is powerless to alleviate the shade's suffering; he and the shade remain on opposite sides of the Law. In the same way, Coetzee's novels bear witness to the tyranny of apartheid while remaining powerless to effect reconciliation. Acutely aware that, like Dante, he is no more than a tourist in an underworld of suffering, Coetzee nevertheless strives to affirm the ground of a certain solidarity, an affirmation that would look forward to a day when reconciliation would truly be possible.[4]

Following the publication of *Doubling the Point*, a wide-ranging collection of essays by and interviews with Coetzee, together with the book-length study, *J. M. Coetzee: South Africa and the Politics of Writing*, David Attwell has emerged as one of the principal apologists for the work of Coetzee. In order to defend him against the influential neo-Marxist critique of Coetzee within South Africa, which accused the novels of failing to represent adequately the material conditions of apartheid,[5] critics such as Attwell and Susan Gallagher have endeavored to *re*historicise Coetzee's fiction by emphasizing its discursive relevance to the time and place in which it was produced. As Attwell himself generously recognizes, his work is indebted to an argument initially put forward by Teresa Dovey in *Lacanian Allegories* that each novel "is positioned within, and deconstructs, a particular subgenre of discourse within the culture" of South Africa (Attwell "Problem" 595).[6] However, this rehistoricization of Coetzee's work sits uneasily with the deliberately unspecific locales of much of Coetzee's fiction and with Coetzee's own insistence on artistic autonomy and on the relationship of "rivalry, even enmity" that pertains between the discourses of literature and history ("Novel" 3). In reading the novels "back into their context," Attwell admits that he is forced to read Coetzee "against the grain" ("J. M. Coetzee" 8), a practice that is somewhat at odds with the meticulous respect for Coetzee's views both as a novelist and as a theorist that he demonstrates throughout the interviews collected in *Doubling the Point.* This chapter attempts neither to dehistoricize nor to rehistoricize Coetzee's fiction, but rather to establish their agonistic, dialectical relation to history.

In a review of *Life and Times of Michael K,* Nadine Gordimer ascribes Coetzee's decision to write what she describes as allegory to a "revulsion" from history.

> It seemed he [chose allegory] out of a kind of opposing desire to hold himself clear of events and their daily, grubby, tragic consequences in which, like everyone else in South Africa, he is up to his neck and about which he had an inner compulsion to write. So here was allegory as stately fastidiousness; or a state of shock. (3)

Gordimer seems to be calling for a mode of realism in which places, events, and people are identifiably South African, as in, for instance, her own novel *Burger's Daughter,* which chronicles the life of a real anti-apartheid activist.[7] Only this direct reference to historical reality, Gordimer seems to imply, rescues the novel from political irrelevance. However, as Rosemary Jolly has argued, Gordimer misunderstands the nature of Coetzee's allegories. The indeterminate settings of the narratives are not simply symptoms of a perverse desire to dehistoricize apartheid; they are instead an attempt both to represent and to contest the historical conditions of apartheid. Jolly thus reads *Waiting for the Barbarians* as a "frontier" novel,[8] "true to the violent domain of conquest in the present . . . but . . . remain[ing] faithful to the future in that its crucial locations are those which suggest the potential for transition" (78). I would add that Coetzee's novels do not provide an allegory of the historical events themselves but of our *relation* to these events. The "state of shock" that Gordimer presents as her diagnosis of the condition from which Coetzee's novels suffer is in fact the novels' own self-diagnosis, the explicit *subject* of each narrative. Rather than pretending that the atrocities of apartheid do not induce a "state of shock" (what would it mean not to be shocked by apartheid?), Coetzee's novels dramatize the problem of relating to a history that defies relation. They attempt to work through their inability to relate (to) the history of apartheid, their inability to "normalize" relations between history and the novel.

As a way of delineating his own agonistic relation to apartheid as a dissident white South African, Coetzee constructs a Lyotardian *differend* between the privileged position of the narrator and the oppressed position of an "other" whose story the narrator seeks to narrate (Parry 40).[9] To put it another way, characters such as Friday in *Foe*, Michael K in *Life and Times of Michael K*, and the barbarian girl in *Waiting for the Barbarians* remain radically incommensurable with the narratives in which they find themselves; unhomely figures of and for alterity, they *embody* precisely that material history of suffering that the narrative is unable to *represent*. Their bodily presence indicates an unmournable, unverbalizable history, a material history that refuses to be translated into words or conjured away by language.

Their status as the racially marked is indicated less by their actual skin color—to which Coetzee makes little or no reference—than by their simultaneous invisibility/visibility. On the one hand, their invisibility as subjects is first of all signaled by their lack of patronyms. Friday and Michael K can only lay claim to first names, while the barbarian girl lacks any name whatsoever.[10] This lack of the name-of-the-father indicates their extrinsic relation to the narrative's symbolic order, to the socio-linguistic sign system that governs human relations. They become the negative image of the Enlightenment subject: a sign of the uncivilized, the inhuman, the native, the infant. On the other hand, the physical disfigurements of these figures of alterity render their status as the objects rather than the subjects of history all too visible. Their disfigurements literally dis-figure or un-name them, marking them as bodies that fail to function as the sign of individual humans. As if to emphasize the absence of an interior life, their history is hieroglyphically inscribed on the surface of their bodies, at precisely the points where we would conventionally expect to be granted access to the depths of an interior life: the eyes and the mouth. Their disfigurements function to deny us this access: Friday's severed tongue and Michael K's harelip constitute literal speech impediments, while the barbarian girl's blindness renders her gaze expressionless and uninterpretable.[11] Their disfigurements do not so much "speak for themselves," as the hackneyed expression goes, as illustrate the impossibility of speaking. They testify to the impossibility of verbal testament.[12]

However, there are also moments in each text where these figures of alterity are more than passive objects, moments of obscure activity that hint at the possibility of a secret interior life. These moments of obscure activity are acts of silent, inconsolable mourning, moments in which these nonsubjects actively bear witness both to a loss of history and to specific histories of loss. Friday scatters petals over the waves to mark the place—or so we are invited to surmise—where his fellow slaves lie submerged. Michael K grows pumpkins and melons in a field fertilized with his mother's ashes. And the barbarian girl—at least in the Magistrate's dreams—gestures toward the site of her loss by constructing a model fort, a replica not only of the fort in which she was tortured but also of the fort of a previous civilization, whose ruins lie buried outside the gates of the present settlement. Like the narrators, we as readers are only able to witness these acts of mourning from afar, unable to say for sure what losses these figures are mourning. Unable to bridge the gap between their world and ours, we are nevertheless overwhelmed by a desire to align ourselves with their mournful gaze and participate in their inconsolable work of mourning.

In all three novels, then, the reader is invited to identify with the narrator's inability to identify with the other. Whereas Gordimer invites her readers to identify with both white and black characters, to imagine these different subject positions, Coetzee erects a kind of color line marking the limits of identification, even while he allows the exact color of his liminal "characters" to remain indeterminate. In representing the interior life of black and white characters, Gordimer operates under the liberal humanist assumption that the novelistic act of empathy can transcend difference. Coetzee's novels implicitly argue that to transcend the other's alterity is to efface that alterity, that the act of empathy is the attempt to imagine the other as the same, as another version of the self. Coetzee's novels insist on the difference of the other in order to explore the impossible task of relating to the other as other.[13] They suggest that the possibility of reconciliation lies not in our ability to *empathize* with the other but rather in an experience of *abjection*, in which, instead of gaining imaginative access to the experience of another subject, one experiences a radical loss of subjectivity, an "experience" (if one can speak of experience in the absence of a subject) that approximates (brings one closer, more proximate to) the experience of being other.[14] Instead of entering into the experience of another, one experiences oneself as other, as abjected beyond the social order that grounds one's subjectivity, as *subjected* to the tyranny of a law that negates one's very existence as an autonomous subject. The act of reading is thus transformed from an act of empathy that takes place firmly within the realm of the human into a radical experience of abjection, in which we are violently expelled from the realm of the human and precipitated toward the realm of the inhuman. For it is only in this underworld of suffering that it becomes momentarily possible to witness, if not to participate in, the "true grief" of the other.

Before embarking on my readings of the novels, I want briefly to explore two theoretical traditions that are central to Coetzee's mode of bearing witness. As a way of foregrounding what I see as the complementary relationship between the ethical stance of Coetzee's novels and their politics, between their relation to alterity and their relation to history, I will suggest that both deconstruction and negative dialectics, often thought of as belonging to antithetical critical traditions, are in fact similarly inconsolable ethico-political practices.[15]

Theodor Adorno's 1962 essay "Commitment" sheds a crucial light on Coetzee's insistence on the autonomy of art. Adorno argues, taking Bertolt Brecht's political allegories as his *exemplum*, that "committed art" (i.e., art that is directly committed to a political cause) is always "poisoned by the untruth of its politics" (187). Because they bear on the external reality of history, the politics of Brecht's plays must necessarily remain "untrue" to the internal reality of the work of art. This is not to say that a work of art cannot contain a political message, but that this message has to be understood first and foremost within the work of art itself, as the sum—or, to use the Marxist term, the *totality*—of its internal relations. For Adorno, only the totality of the work of art has any relation to the society in which it is produced: like Georg Lukács, who also opposed Brechtian theatre but for very different reasons, Adorno sees the work of art as revealing the relations of production, the economic forces, that structure reality. However, opposing Lukács' adherence to the mimesis of realism—an adherence that, as Susan Gallagher points out, is still in evidence in the neo-Marxist dismissal of Coetzee (Gallagher 29)—Adorno argues that art should provide a "negative image" of society, one that stands in dialectical contradiction to society, as its critique. For Adorno, there can be no accommodation between the spheres of life and art, no shared or homologous content, even though there is nothing in art "which did not originate in the empirical reality from which it breaks free" (190).

It is no coincidence that the two artists that Adorno cites as having produced this "negative image" of society are the same two authors that have been widely seen—not least by Coetzee himself—as Coetzee's literary predecessors: Franz Kafka and Samuel Beckett. Nevertheless, when art is called upon to declare its commitment to the revolutionary struggle—in 1930s Germany or 1980s South Africa—it is unsurprising that Lukácsian realism comes to seem a good deal more satisfactory than the hermetic work of a Kafka or a Coetzee, in all its fastidious refusal not to be "poisoned by the untruth of politics." Have Coetzee's novels merely afforded a welcome respite from the day-to-day realities of apartheid? Or have they instead provided some way of working through the history from which they appear to abstain?

To answer this question, we need to return briefly to Adorno's essay, the last part of which deals with the question of whether it is possible—and indeed ethical—to produce art after Auschwitz. Standing by his earlier pronouncement that "to write lyric poetry after Auschwitz is barbaric" (188), Adorno nevertheless agrees with Hans Magnus Enzensberger's reply that "literature must resist this verdict":

> The abundance of real suffering tolerates no forgetting; Pascal's theological saying, *on ne doit plus dormir*, must be secularized. Yet this suffer-

ing, what Hegel called consciousness of adversity, also demands the con-
tinued existence of art while it prohibits it; it is now virtually in art alone
that suffering can find its own voice, consolation, without being betrayed
by it. (188)

Without wishing to posit an historical equivalence between the *shoah* and
apartheid, I would argue that Coetzee's art seeks for itself the task of bearing
witness to "the abundance of real suffering" engendered by apartheid—and
more broadly by the history of colonialism, the larger context within which
Coetzee insists South African apartheid must be understood. The dialectical
movement of Adorno's thinking captures the agonistic position that Coetzee
is forced to adopt. To create art seems blasphemous in the face of excessive
suffering but, equally well, art may be the only means of remembering this
suffering, of giving "suffering its own voice." Art cannot help but betray its
intentions, in its translation of that which it seeks to remember into art: "The
moral of this art, not to forget for a single instant, slithers into its opposite"
(189). In an attempt to arrest the slide from remembrance to forgetting, Coetzee creates works of art that attempt to remember their own inability to
remember, narratives that draw attention to their own incompletion, the
silence at their core.

Like the work of Beckett and Kafka, Coetzee's novels attempt to remain
speechless before history (Adorno 191). Their fundamental position is that of
Mrs. Curren in *Age of Iron*, called upon to witness and to name the destruction of a township, "the crime being committed in front of [her] eyes": "'To
speak of this'—[she] waved a hand over the bush, the smoke, the filth litter-
ing the path—'you would need the tongue of a god'" (91). Like Coetzee's novels, her speech is a mode of remaining silent. In an interview, Coetzee himself
underlines his own speechlessness by speaking of how he is "overwhelmed,"
how "his thinking is thrown into confusion and helplessness by the fact of suffering in the world" (*Doubling the Point*, 248). And Adorno ends his essay by
invoking exactly the same figure of the artist overwhelmed, incapacitated,
before the spectacle of history, in his reference to Paul Klee's *Angelus Novus*.
In earlier sketches, he tells us, the figure was intended as a cartoon of Kaiser
Wilhelm, but the final version, owned by Walter Benjamin, "flies far
beyond . . . any emblem of caricature or commitment" (194)—beyond direct
political reference and a politics of blame toward an acceptance of an unavoid-
able implication in history.

In Benjamin's perhaps too familiar description, the Angel sees history
not as "a chain of events," as an immediately recognizable narrative of "'the
way it really was'" (255), but instead as "one single catastrophe which keeps
piling wreckage upon wreckage . . . in front of his feet. The Angel would like
to stay, awaken the dead, and make whole what has been smashed" but is

instead ceaselessly blown into the future (257). On the one hand, then, Benjamin's Angel is a true "historical materialist," refusing to transcend the materiality of history, refusing to explain away the rubble of the past by turning it into a coherent historical discourse.[16] On the other, the Angel of History is still an angel, one who would like to redeem history by making whole what has been smashed. Although he is unable to carry out such a task, his thwarted desire is a mode of remembrance that recognizes each historical fragment as nonetheless waiting for—in want of—redemption, as part of an historical present that is "shot through with chips of Messianic time" (263).

In secularizing Pascal, Adorno implicitly recognizes the religious origins of his ethic of remembrance. Coetzee does likewise in his reading of Dante's encounter with the shade. Benjamin comes from the opposite direction, supplementing the secular Marxist tradition with an explicitly sacred ethic of remembrance, drawn from the Jewish Kabbala. All three make reference to religion in order to suggest the relation of memory to the future. Coetzee's novels, in their refusal to transcend the materiality of history, constitute works of remembrance that "point towards a practice from which they abstain: the creation of a just life" (Adorno 194).[17] In anticipation of the end of apartheid, they labor, as Derrida would say, "in memory of the hope" of a just future.

Adorno's concern with how art might remember suffering without forgetting it parallels Derrida's concern with the ethics of representation. In "Cogito and the History of Madness," for instance, Derrida argues that it is impossible to write a history of madness without reimprisoning madness within a discourse of reason. Like Adorno, he recognizes the inevitability of betraying those to whom one seeks to do justice, and in so doing, betraying one's own project. However, this act of imprisonment or betrayal is never total. The same movement that reimprisons madness within reason also provokes a crisis *within* reason. Madness itself, in its absolute difference from reason, exceeds Foucault's grasp but nevertheless installs itself at the center of Foucault's project as a silence that must remain, in Foucault's text as in any other, a silence. If, as Foucault argues, "madness is the absence of a work" (qtd. in Derrida 54), then madness can only reside in the absence of *Foucault's* work. Foucault's work succeeds precisely where it fails: silence becomes not only "the work's limit [but also its] profound resource" (55), its most successful way of delineating the history of madness.

The same argument governs Derrida's analysis of the work of mourning. Whereas successful or "healthy" mourning is the assimilation or integration of loss into consciousness, unsuccessful or unhealthy mourning, what Freud termed melancholia, is marked by the failure to integrate loss into consciousness (the secret denial that the loss has even occurred). For Derrida, it is precisely in this failure of integration that mourning becomes ethical. While successful mourning constitutes an idealizing "consumption" of the dead, the absorption of difference into the self-same, failed mourning "leav[es] the other his alterity, respecting thus his infinite remove" (*Mémoires* 6). In his foreword to Karl Abraham and Maria Torok's *The Wolf Man's Magic Word: A Cryptonomy*, Derrida describes this failure of integration as an "encryptment" of the dead within the living: "Cryptic incorporation marks an effect of impossible or refused mourning" (xxi). Both senses of the "cryptic" are drawn on here: the dead remain secretly entombed within—internal to but sealed off from—the consciousness of the living, and they also remain enigmatic, coded, untranslated. The fixation on the body of the dead evoked by the idea of burial is further emphasized by the term in*corp*oration. While successful mourning is a movement of transcendence that allows the soul or spirit of the dead a kind of secular afterlife in the memory of the living, unsuccessful mourning is the failure to move beyond the corpse, beyond the fact of physical death. While successful mourning is a movement of *idealization* in which the dead are abstracted into a *memory*, unsuccessful mourning *incorporates* the dead as a foreign body, as a material *trace*.

In *Mémoires for Paul de Man*, Derrida links his critique of mourning to his critique of Foucault's project by paralleling successful mourning with the historicist desire to recover the past.[18] The historicist narrative attempts to do for the collective memory what the language of mourning—elegy, epitaph, ode, obituary, oration—attempts to do for the individual memory, namely obtain mastery over the past by translating it into a recognizable form. In seeking to come to terms with death, the language of mourning seeks to memorialize or commemorate the dead by translating loss into words, silence into speech. Similarly, the historicist project seeks to render the past legible, to translate the past into discourse—and in so doing it must necessarily efface the difference of history, what Paul de Man referred to as "the materiality of actual history" (de Man, qtd. in *Mémoires* 30).

I find de Man's phrase useful because it reverses the usual assumption that historicism deals with material history while poststructuralist discourses such as deconstruction reduce everything to "textuality" or even ahistorical abstraction. In fact, as we shall see in Coetzee's fiction, it is only in the breakdown of historicizing narrative that we are able to glimpse the materiality of history. What de Man calls "true mourning" is precisely the failure to assimilate the dead into an historical narrative, precisely the refusal of this gesture of appropriation. Successful mourning enables the past to be assimilated or digested; one remembers in order to be consoled, ultimately in order to forget. By contrast, true mourning confronts an indigestible past, a past that can never be fully remembered or forgotten.[19]

To say that Coetzee's bodies mark the site of "actual material history" is to recognize on the one hand that they are intensely material or "substantial" bodies, "humanity" reduced to a meaningless "pile of blood, bone and meat that is unhappy" (*Waiting for the Barbarians* 85), and on the other, that they are the site of a loss or a disappearance, that far from housing a soul or a subject, they contain "a story with a hole in it" (*Michael K* 110) through which the subject seems to disappear. Coetzee's bodies attempt to mourn their own loss, to tell the story of their own eclipse. And in so doing, they open out onto a wider history of loss, a history that is not their own and that indeed cannot be owned, a history that *ungrounds* them as individual subjects.

This, then, is why I would describe Coetzee's novels as works of failed or inconsolable mourning. Derrida's analysis of mourning sheds light on Coetzee's decision not to grant his figures of alterity patronyms—as a refusal to historicize the suffering of the dispossessed, a refusal to allow the reader to digest this suffering and then forget it. While naming makes representation—and thus mourning—possible by enabling us to speak of others in their absence, to remember and ultimately to forget them, the "failed" names of Friday, Michael K, and the barbarian girl arrest this process of representation and mourning. Precisely because they are not adequately named and thus remembered, they cannot be forgotten. Precisely because they are not fully individuated characters, they serve as reminders of all those who have been denied humanity, reminders of the history of barbarity that, as Benjamin famously noted, underwrites the history of civilization.[20] Coetzee's novels seek to find a way of relating to this "underwritten" history, this history that is simultaneously internal and external to the history of civilization, central yet excluded. Because they are themselves narratives, part of the history of civilization, they must attempt to relate to that which they themselves exclude, to that which they are themselves forced to under/overwrite. Their metafictional contortions are a way of gesturing toward their own excluded interior, their own encrypting of the realm of material history.

My reading of these novels will not attempt to decrypt, to render legible, this cryptic history. For this would be merely to repeat the futile attempts of their narrators, Susan, the doctor, and the Magistrate respectively. Rather, I will attempt to chart a movement that takes place in the wake of the failure to read Coetzee's figures of alterity, the failure to recover a history. In other words, I will attempt to trace both a story of disappearance and a disappearance of story, to follow Coetzee's figures of alterity as they seem to exit their own narratives and gesture not only toward a forgotten history but also toward the history of a Forgetting.

FRIDAY'S SILENCE

Foe, Coetzee's rewriting of *Robinson Crusoe*, differs from other postcolonial rewritings of canonical texts in that it does not attempt to recover the voice of the colonized other. Rather, it strives to remember the silencing of this other, the history of Forgetting of which Defoe's novel is itself a part. In Defoe's original narrative, Friday is passed over or lost as a subject from the moment that, having been rescued from his fellow "cannibals," he lays his head under Crusoe's foot and has this gesture interpreted by Crusoe as "a token of swearing to be my slave for ever" (Defoe 200). Coetzee's text marks the violence of this act of ventriloquism by representing Friday as always already silenced, as unable to speak because his tongue has been ripped out of his mouth.

Instead of recovering the voice of Friday, Coetzee imports his narrator, Susan Barton, from another of Defoe's novels, *Roxana*. Susan arrives on the island in the last year of Cruso's island narrative.[21] She refuses to pass over the fact of Friday's silence and comes to suspect that it was Cruso who cut out Friday's tongue. However, this and other acts of what Coetzee, with a nod toward Freud, terms "speculative history" underline the way in which she comes after Friday's "othering" and thus can only ever be—like the reader—a belated witness to his suffering.[22] She discovers the impossibility of penetrating "the silence surrounding Friday" (142). Nevertheless, as in *Madness and Civilization*, this silence comes to take up residence in the absence(s) of Susan's narrative. Susan comes to feel that her own account of what happened on the island, which, on returning to England, she tries to persuade Foe to write, is rendered radically incomplete without the story of Friday's "mut(e)ilation" (Begam 119). As she tells Foe, "the shadow whose lack you feel [in my story] is there: it is the loss of Friday's tongue" (117).

How is it that Susan is able to encrypt Friday's story within her own? How is it that Friday's silence comes to haunt the center of *her* narrative? What are the motives and consequences of this act of encryptment? On the one hand, Susan is guilty of a violent appropriation of Friday as cultural capital; in becoming Friday's self-appointed guardian, she merely takes over Cruso's position as Friday's owner. As her repeated failures to bring Friday to speech indicate, Friday's story is as sealed off as ever, and like Cruso before her, she finds herself ventriloquizing Friday's desire, only this time it is the desire to be free, rather than enslaved, that is attributed to Friday: "Friday's desires are plain to me. He desires to be liberated, as I do" (148). On the other, her insistence that the story she has to tell is the story of what happened on the island and not the alternative story of *Roxana*, her refusal to be the central protagonist of her own novel, constitutes a mode of self-negation: she refuses to acknowledge as her own the child who dogs her every move once she returns to England precisely because to accept this narrative of loss and restitution (that of *Roxana*) would be to render her own narrative complete and thus leave no room for the story of Friday's silencing. Her refusal to recognize herself as a mother is a power play that allows her to claim an alternative position as the "father" of Friday's story but, in refusing the restoration, the consolation, of the child, she is able to remain incomplete, inconsolable.

Spivak usefully suggests that we read Susan as "the agent of other-directed ethics" (164). My emphasis on the work of mourning leads me to suggest that by positioning Friday's story as a hole in her own narrative, Susan allows the emptiness of her own narrative to bear witness to Friday's loss of history—and to the wider history of loss to which the "fact" of his mut(e)ilation itself bears witness. I place quotation marks around the word *fact* in order to emphasize the double reference of Friday's mut(e)ilation, as something that does not actually occur in Defoe's narrative, but which undeniably did occur during the material history of slavery that the narrative occludes. Coetzee does not attempt to remember or recover this material history, not so much because this history is not available, but because he is interested in how this history has been occluded, in how it was possible to write a novel such as *Robinson Crusoe*, to (re)write the barbarity of slavery as benevolent paternalism.

But Coetzee is interested in more than a *critique* of this forgetting of history. The narrative also actively bears witness to this occlusion of material history. This process of bearing witness is structured as a *mise en abîme*, in which the hole in Susan's subjectivity reveals the hole in Friday's subjectivity, which in turn reveals the historyless limbo to which Friday's ancestors have been consigned. This structure is set up early on in the novel: having allowed Cruso to "do as he wished" with her body (thereby negating herself by suspending the question of her own desire), Susan then interrogates herself about the nature of this abject experience:

> We yield to a stranger's embrace or give ourselves to the waves; for the blink of an eyelid our vigilance relaxes; we are asleep; and when we awake we have lost the direction of our lives. What are these blinks of an eyelid, against which the only defence is an eternal and inhuman wakefulness? Might they not be cracks and chinks through which another voice, other voices, speak in our lives? (30)

Immediately after this passage, Susan witnesses Friday floating near the shore on a log. She initially assumes he is fishing, but then sees him scattering petals and buds onto the surface of the water; she concludes that Friday is "making an offering to the god of the waves . . . or performing some other such superstitious observance" (31).

Coming straight after Susan's meditation on her moment of abnegation, it is impossible not to see Friday's actions as his own mode of "giving [him]self to the waves." However, it is also one of the only moments in the novel in which we gain a glimpse of Friday's "true" nature, one of the only moments in which he is not acting under compulsion; suggestively straddling the log (it is elsewhere hinted that he may be castrated), it is as if he is momentarily free to articulate his own desire.[23] But as we shall see in *Life and Times of Michael K*, this desire is itself a desire for negation, the dangerous, life-threatening, even death-desiring desire of those unable to sever their emotional ties to the dead: *if*, as Foe and Susan come to suspect, Friday is floating above a slave ship, the watery grave of his fellow slaves, then we can read Friday's scattering of petals as an act of inconsolable mourning, as the sign of either an inability or a refusal to recover from history.

However, I highlight the word *if* in order to indicate that we are in the realm of "speculative history." My "interpretation" of Friday's act relies not only on Susan and Foe's subsequent speculations, but also on the veracity of Susan's account of the scene, on the truth of her witnessing. Because the scene follows directly on from her meditation on self-forgetfulness, it as if the scene itself is experienced as a *dream:* we are only able to witness Friday's own act of bearing witness through a crack in Susan's subjectivity, through a lapse in her own being in which she has momentarily forgotten the narrative of her self. Of course, dreams are notoriously the scene of a certain wish fulfillment; Friday may well be acting under compulsion after all, may well be merely doing Susan's psychic bidding. But, as we shall see, the novel keeps open the possibility of another understanding of dreams as the place where our own desire is suspended and "other voices make themselves heard in our lives."

This alternative interpretation of dreams is articulated later on in the novel. While they are lying beside each other in Foe's bed, Foe asks Susan about the function and value of dreaming: "Would we be better or worse . . . if we were no longer to descend nightly into ourselves and meet . . . our darker selves, and other phantoms too" (137–38)? The final encounter with Friday will make it clear that this is a deliberately racial reference, but what Foe (Coetzee) has in mind at this juncture, I would suggest, is the idea that a descent into the self is ultimately an encounter with that which is irreducibly other within the self. To follow out Foe's reasoning: it is this nightly encounter with our own encrypted otherness that enables us to be "better" rather than "worse," to relate—ethically—to the otherness of those we encounter in our *daily* lives.[24]

Foe then goes on to speak of another "descent"—Dante's descent into hell—and of grief: "One of the souls was weeping. 'Do not suppose, mortal,' said this soul addressing him, 'that because I am not substantial these tears you behold are not the tears of a true grief'" (138). As I noted earlier, the soul, addressing Dante, and also, of course, the reader, makes an appeal based on the truth-value of his grief, and in so doing his tears acquire a certain materiality that causes Dante to reciprocate in kind, offering his own tears as a sign of his own substantial grief. Susan's response to this, "True grief, but whose? . . . The ghost's or the Italian's" (138), reminds us of the privileges of authorship and of the gap that separates Dante's remorse from that of the shade. Nevertheless, Foe—and the narrative itself, as the ending makes clear—cannot quite give up this dream of a place where it would be possible to shed truly reciprocal tears.

As a descent into the self, as a loss of self-consciousness, dreams mark the encounter with what is ordinarily, in our waking lives, most *external* to us—namely, the pain of others—as something *internal* to our own consciousness.[25] For Coetzee, most notably in *Waiting for the Barbarians,* dreams are the site of a transmission of pain, of an identification with the suffering of the other that is only possible because it takes place outside the realm of self-knowledge. While in their waking lives Coetzee's characters encounter the limits of empathic identification with other subjects, their dream lives open up the possibility of an abject identification with the other as other.

Julia Kristeva describes abjection as the experience of being thrown out of oneself, literally ab-jected, a "descent into the foundations of the symbolic construct" that guarantees our individuation and separation as subjects, a re-experiencing, in reverse, of the moment of our separation, in order to arrive at a place where self and other are "inseparable" (*Powers of Horror* 18). But this "contamination" of self and other is precisely the opposite of the transcendent movement of an empathic identification. Like Derrida's concept of failed mourning, Kristeva's concept of abjection is directed against the Platonic tradition in which matter is idealized and the other absorbed into the self. Abjection is a reduction of the self to the body in which the body becomes radically defamiliarized, bereft of the cultural codes by which we usually recognize it. The abject body is auto-referential: no longer operating as a sign of the human, it accrues its own weight or pathos and becomes an image of its own pain. "Significance," Kristeva writes, "is indeed inherent in the human body" (10).

Echoing Kristeva's description, Coetzee's narrator describes the extra-textual, extrahistorical location of the last pages of *Foe* as "a place where bodies are their own signs" (155). As I suggested in the introduction, the image comes into its own as an image of death. Outside the realm of representation, the image can at last realize itself not as a mimetic imitation of something else, but as itself. Here, in this underworld, this world of death, the image discovers its abject vocation, what Derrida describes as its "being-for-death" ("By Force of Mourning" 176). The last movement of the novel reenacts Dante's descent into a world of bodily pain and stages its own abject encounter in which the boundary between self and other is precisely *not* transcended, but instead *materialized.* In the wake of the narrative's failure to bring Friday to speech, the abject sight of Friday's body/corpse reduces the narrative to silence, to that speechlessness before history that Adorno argues is proper to the modern work of art.

This final movement is in fact two movements, two descents, narrated without quotation marks, as if Susan had relinquished her hold on the narrative, as if this were not a narrative at all, as if in order to enter "the home of Friday," one would have to give up all claims to narration. On the first descent the nonnarrator enters an unnamed house, forces open Friday's clenched teeth, and hears "the faintest faraway roar . . . of the waves in a seashell . . . the sounds of the island" (154). If this first descent restages Susan's frustrated desire to bring Friday to speech, the second descent is a repetition of the first—but with the difference that the nonnarrator becomes involved in an act of reading. After identifying the house as that of "Daniel Defoe, Author" (155) (and thereby entering a house of fiction), he picks up Susan's abandoned manuscript and begins to read it: "Bringing the candle nearer, I read the first words of the tall, looping script: 'Dear Mr Foe, At last I could row no further.' With a sigh, making barely a splash, I slip overboard" and subsequently "under the water" (155), as if he were diving through the hole in Susan's narrative— and thus through the hole in Friday's history—where he comes upon a shipwreck, the true "home of Friday" (157). To read the text—or rather the thing itself, the actual material manuscript—is to be led beyond the text, as if it were possible to follow the image's lead, its silent movement toward a world beyond the world of representation.

Kristeva describes abjection as the communication of a nonverbal speech: "[a] sad analytic silence hover[s] above a strange foreign discourse, which strictly speaking shatters verbal communication . . . it is necessary that the analyst's interpretative speech . . . be affected by it in order to be analytical" (30). On this second descent, as the nonnarrator attempts to prise open Friday's mouth, he dislodges a stream of bubbles: "Each syllable, as it comes out, is caught and filled with water and diffused" (157). These strange, foreign syllables constitute a material language, the language, as it were, of material history, the bodily sign of a substantial grief. They function as a form of metonymic remembrance, in their silent recollection of the modalities of Friday's silence, of the Os that Friday is said to utter as a mode of prayer in *Robinson Crusoe;* of the "walking eyes" that Friday draws on the slate that Foe gives him (147); of the aporia of Friday's history as he traces it on the surface of the water; of the hole in Susan's narrative, which is also described as an "eye" or a "mouth" (141); and even of the island itself.

The last line of the novel "wakes" us out of the narrative, out of the dream of being able to encounter our "darker selves," but nonetheless suggests a possible "transference" of the affective bubbles of Friday's nonspeech into the tears of the nonnarrator—and perhaps the reader: "His mouth opens. From inside him comes a slow stream, without breath, without interruption. [. . .] Soft and cold, dark and unending, it beats against my eyelids, against the skin of my face" (157). The nonnarrator's eyelids function as a threshold. The bubbles of

Friday's lament cannot occupy the same space as the nonnarrator's tears, tears that announce the cessation of the dream, the moment of severance, the irrevocable moment of waking in which we are forced to recognize the gulf that lies between a privileged world where we may dream of "slipp[ing] overboard" into a text and the realm of "actual material history."

MICHAEL K'S VIGIL

Coetzee's novels, I have suggested, labor in memory of the hope of a just future. Although *Life and Times of Michael K* seems initially to function as an apocalyptic projection of what might have happened in South Africa had the National Party not been forced to grant free elections (civil war), it ultimately functions as an affirmation, as a promise of the survival of human nature beyond the end of history and civilization. Critics have rightly read the novel in terms of an opposition between nature and culture. However, even the most sensitive of these readings have tended to account for this opposition by positing an ambivalence at the heart of Coetzee's novelistic sensibility. Michael Valdez Moses, for instance, sees Coetzee's work as oscillating between a Rousseauistic nostalgia for the natural state of man and a Nietzschean self-reflexive scepticism that realizes the impossibility of such a return. Moses fails to make sense of this tension beyond suggesting that the scepticism tempers, or even cancels out, the nostalgia. Rita Barnard also focuses on an opposition between nostalgia and scepticism, but suggests, via a reference to Adorno, that Coetzee's nostalgia is directed toward the future. She narrowly misses the revolutionary potential of Adorno's negative dialectics by attributing a naive utopian dimension to this "nostalgia," concluding by suggesting that Coetzee's novels look forward to a time in which "the novel could again invoke, not ironically, but lyrically, the 'country ways' of the pastoral" (Barnard 55). To return to such a mode of representation would constitute another forgetting, another denial of history. Against such utopian nostalgia, and in line with Adorno's sense of the dangers of aestheticization, Coetzee's novels instead strive never to forget: they certainly look forward to the possibility of justice or freedom, or in the South African context to a day in which humanity would no longer be stunted by the unnatural or inhuman relations of apartheid; however, such a day is predicated not on a utopian nostalgia but on our capacity to live in remembrance.[26]

    Nevertheless, Barnard's otherwise excellent article is a useful exploration of the tension between Coetzee's critique of South African pastoralism and his own pastoral hankerings. In his critical study *White Writing* (1988), Coetzee shows how Afrikaner pastoralism functions as an ideological evacuation of the landscape, an erasure of the native presence and labor. As Barnard puts it, "this secret displacement is the historical precondition of the Afrikaner's idyllic map of rural homesteading," by which he is able to claim that the land belongs to him and he to it. Although Barnard later acutely suggests that K "finds a way to reclaim displacement, invisibility, tracklessness, as a form of freedom" (52–53), early on in her essay she suggests that Coetzee's response to this forgetting is a simple act of recovery: "Coetzee renders visible the places that the system would rather keep out of sight and mind" (36). Had this been Coetzee's strategy, he would surely have written a realist antipastoral, which would have laid bare the material conditions of rural labor. Instead, I would argue that, rather than rendering visible that which was excluded, the novel exposes the mechanism of exclusion; it remembers not native labor itself but the Forgetting of that labor.

The novel begins as if it were indeed possible to relate the life and times of Michael K, as if it were possible to write a subaltern history. However, by the end of the first section, K has eluded the surveillance of the seemingly omniscient third person narrative, abdicated his position as subject, and found a way out of his life and times. Attempting to become no more than "a speck upon the surface of the earth" (97), K digs himself a hole in the Karoo and enters a state of hibernation in which his body begins to disappear, in mute articulation of his refusal to be remembered, his desire only to be forgotten.

After he is dug up and taken to a military hospital, a doctor takes up the narrative, and with it, the task of memory. Finding K's vanishing act a scandalous affront to his scientific knowledge—"The body, I had been taught, wants only to live" (164)—he attempts to feed, to "remember," K against his will. K attempts to question the nature of the doctor's desire: "Why do you want to make me fat? why fuss over me, why am I so important?" to which the doctor replies by asserting the law of memory: ". . . you are not important. But that does not mean you are forgotten. No one is forgotten" (135). And then, in his longest speech of the novel, K places the forgotten life of his mother against the doctor's claim that no one is forgotten:

> "My mother worked all her life long," he said. "She scrubbed other people's floors, she cooked for them, she washed their dishes. She washed their dirty clothes. She scrubbed the bath after them. She went on her knees and cleaned the toilet. But when she was old and sick they forgot her. They put her away out of sight. When she died they threw her in the fire. They gave me an old box of ash and told me, 'Here is your mother, take her away, she is no good to us.'" (136)

This passage is key to understanding K's own bid to be forgotten as a mode of remembrance, as an attempt to identify with the way in which his mother has been forgotten. The doctor is almost right to suggest that K is not so much on hunger strike as merely holding out for the food that he grew for himself in the veld. K does indeed crave the pumpkins grown on a farm that may or may not be that of his mother's half-remembered childhood, in a field fertilized by what may or may not be her ashes. But we know that this food offers K little physical nourishment; it only assists him in his attempt to disappear. For in eating the pumpkins, he incorporates not so much his mother as the absence of a mother whom even he cannot remember. Shortly after her death he finds that "he did not miss her, except insofar as he had missed her all his life" (34). His time on the farm is an attempt to identify not so much with his mother's idealized memory of freedom as a child as with the unfreedom of her forgotten life as a domestic servant. He attempts to live in remembrance of his mother by eating the nothing of her existence.

Another way of putting this would be to say that K's body attempts to follow the path of his mother's disappearance. At the beginning of the novel, K's mother seems to be dying of swollen limbs, almost as if her body is rebelling against the hidden, forgotten nature of her life, almost as if her body—and its history of suffering—is clamouring for remembrance. Thus K's filial devotion, his attempt to transport her back to the home of her childhood, is already a labor of mourning. As he wheels her out through the suburbs of Cape Point and into the veld, he has already begun to grapple with the weight of her history, with a history that has grown, to borrow a term from *Foe*, substantial. And when his mother, grown impossibly large, is suddenly translated into a tiny packet of ashes, how could this experience not prove traumatic for K? How could it not prove to be a crisis of remembrance? In reducing his mother's swollen body to ashes, it is as if the hospital has refused to recognize her demand to be remembered and actively consigned her to historical oblivion.

Thus K's cultivation of his mother's ashes, his dogged refusal to forget a mother that he cannot remember, is not just the working out of a private or personal grief. It is a protest against the state's refusal to remember; it is an attempt to remember a whole class of people that the state would rather forget, a people whom they would rather lock out of sight in camps, as a fellow worker explains to Michael, a people who they would have "come on tiptoe in the middle of the night like fairies and do their work, dig their gardens, wash their pots, and be gone in the morning leaving everything nice and clean" (82). K's labor as a gardener is thus simultaneously an attempt to identify with his mother's disappearance and a protest against this disappearance, a protest against the Forgetting of labor. The swelling of the pumpkins, which parallels the swelling of his mother's limbs, recalls this ambivalence. On the one hand, they assist K in his attempt to disappear; on the other, as they begin to ripen they threaten to betray his secret, nocturnal labor (he only tends to his pumpkins at night, for fear of being observed), as if they too were clamoring for remembrance.

K himself understands his gardening as a mode of remembering the future, as an attempt, in a time of war, to "keep gardening alive, or at least the idea of gardening; because once that cord was broken, the earth would grow hard and forget her children" (109). K's own vocabulary, together with the description of the two hills that form the crevice into which he burrows as "plump breasts" (100), makes it clear that his desire to maintain a connection with the land is intimately bound up with his refusal to sever the ties between himself and his dead mother. His labor of love fulfills not only his filial responsibilities to his mother but also his paternal responsibilities: he thinks of his pumpkins not only as the earth's but also as his own children (113). Melancholia is thus rewritten as ethical commitment, a commitment that, like Coetzee's commitment to his art, is also a refusal to acknowledge what others see as the more immediate political concerns of the present, an "untimely" refusal to accept that "the time for gardening [or pastoral novels] was when the war was over" (109). Interestingly, Moses also makes this connection between K's commitment to his gardening and Coetzee's commitment to his art, but simultaneously seeks to qualify the radical force of this desire to live outside history: "Just as K must ultimately acknowledge the hold that society has upon him, and the transitory and effectively powerless state of the solitary reverie, so too must Coetzee acknowledge that the world of fiction is not fully autonomous or immune to external forces" (153). Moses's tone is unmistakably that of the Enlightenment: one can momentarily entertain dreams of freedom, but the mature, rational citizen will eventually realize that the true nature of freedom is responsibility. However, the tone, the alternative *ethos*, of Michael K and his author is equally unmistakably that of a Romanticism that marks a radical break with—which refuses to acknowledge—the moralism of the Enlightenment: their ethical understanding stems not from maturity but from the radical innocence of the child. As Coetzee puts it in *Waiting for the Barbarians*, children "come into the world bringing with them the memory of justice," a memory that is perpetually at odds with the "world of laws" (139). The radical force of this memory is that—and this is what Moses, speaking from the perspective of civilization and from within its teleological timeframe, misses—it is not the solitary reverie but the way of the world that is revealed as "transitory." K tends to his garden because he recognizes that human nature is not wholly determined by the idea of civilization; he waits for the end of the time of history as the beginning of the time of the human.

The strength of K's resolve becomes clear in the final section of the novel, in which K disappears from the military hospital, returns to his mother's room at Cape Point, and then imagines—at the point of his own death, in the transferential space of a final reverie—returning to the abandoned farm, pushing a fellow tramp back to Prince Albert in another wheelbarrow. This imagined journey, this dream of freedom in which K finally succeeds, perhaps, in taking his mother home, needs to be placed alongside that of the doctor, who imagines following K out into the veld in order to discover the secret of his existence. As in *Foe,* Coetzee presents us with a double ending, a double journey. Just as the final narrator of *Foe* seeks to confirm his speculations about the shipwreck, the doctor runs after K to seek confirmation of his speculations about K's "sacred garden": "Am I right. . . . Have I understood you? If I am right hold up your right hand; if I am wrong, hold up your left" (167). Only after K has outrun this attempt to reimprison him within the confines of narrative is he free to imagine, at the moment of death, the disclosure of his secret life, a life lived in memory of the hope of a day in which it would truly be possible to live. But this act of disclosure itself remains a dream. K imagines revealing himself to a fellow tramp who is only present in the narrative as a trace, as the smell of whoever last slept on K's final resting place of cardboard: it is only possible to reveal himself, or so it would seem, to his own spirit or "shade."

THE CRIES COMING FROM THE GRANARY

Life and Times of Michael K is the negative image not only of South African history but also of its fictional predecessor, *Waiting for the Barbarians.* Each novelistic project collapses into the other. In *Life and Times of Michael K* the attempt to relate the "interior life" of an outcast suddenly finds itself external to this life, forced to take up the excluded, frustrated position of a narrator who cannot fathom the secret of K's existence. In *Waiting for the Barbarians* the Magistrate's frustrated attempts to go beneath the surface of the barbarian girl's tortured body suddenly give way to an interior dream life containing intimations of a life beyond the confines of Empire. A hidden passage connects the Magistrate's desire to discover what happened in the intimate recesses of the torture chamber, the secret life that takes place at the heart of Empire, with the doctor's attempts to discover the secret of K's impossible existence in the wide open spaces of the veld. Both novels reveal the dialectical hinge between nature and culture, the moment where nature reveals itself as the ground of our humanity, and culture as the ground of our inhumanity, as that which renders us inhuman. It is this disjunction between the time of nature and the time of history that fuels K's desire to live in "a pocket outside time" (60) and the Magistrate's desire to "live outside the history that Empire imposes on its subjects" (154). Each novel works out the same dialectic between confinement and freedom, the present and the future, the pain of the captive body and the "bliss" (*Michael K* 68) of the liberated body, a bliss that nevertheless "remembers," bears an uncanny resemblance to, the suffering of the body in pain.

Waiting for the Barbarians dramatizes the question of how to address oneself to a history that remains inaccessible even in the very moment of its occurrence. Implicated as readers in the Magistrate's first person narration, the novel forces us to consider our own relation to the history of torture, as part of a history that takes place "out of sight."[27] For Coetzee, torture is part of the same history of state-sanctioned forgetting that Michael K seeks to protest:

> The response of South Africa's legislators to what disturbs them is usu-
> ally to order it out of sight. If people are starving, let them starve far away
> in the bush, where their thin bodies will not be a reproach. If they have
> no work, if they migrate to the cities, let there be roadblocks, let there be
> curfews, let there be laws against vagrancy, begging and squatting, and let
> offenders be locked away so that no one has to see or hear them. If the
> black townships are in flames, let cameras be banned from them. (*Dou-
> bling the Point* 361)

However, as in *Life and Times of Michael K,* Coetzee's project is not simply to render these things visible. Rather than attempting to recover a history of tor-ture, the novel is a dramatization of the consequences of the state's attempt to forget or conceal this history—and of how we might learn to live in remem-brance of this Forgetting. In other words, it seeks to show how this Forgetting of torture is not merely one instance of forgetfulness among others but one that is *constitutive* of life under apartheid.

The originary event or "primal scene" that drives the narrative and to which the narrative endlessly seeks to return is thus not a direct experience of torture but rather the attempt *not* to register that torture is taking place.[28] As Coetzee himself writes, the novel is "about the impact of the torture chamber on the life of a man of conscience" (*Doubling the Point* 363). The torture chamber—not torture itself, but the fact of its occurrence in a "dark chamber," sealed off from the outside world—is experienced by the Magistrate as a blow not only to his conscience, to his ethical well-being, but also to his (self-) con-sciousness, to his experience of himself as a finite, individuated, self-sufficient being. His attempt to deny having heard the cries produces a crisis. At first he claims: "Of the screaming which people afterwards claim to have heard com-ing from the granary, I hear nothing" (5). But this denial later modulates into an active refusal to hear: "I stopped my ears" (9), thence into an admission of failure: "I would like to be able to stop my ears" (21), and finally into confu-sion: "straining my ears to hear or not to hear sounds of violence" (22). It is as if he has experienced a blow that has shattered that part of the mind that func-tions as "a protective shield against stimuli" (Freud, *Beyond the Pleasure Prin-ciple* 298). No longer able to insulate himself against the suffering of others, he is from now on perpetually haunted by the awareness that, as he puts it (quoting Freud), "Somewhere, always, a child is being beaten" (80).

The Magistrate's failure not to hear the cries coming from the gra-nary thus marks the end of what Lacan would call, parodying Descartes, his self-certainty, and the beginning of an ethics based on the certainty not of one's own existence but of the existence of others.[29] The cries are the signs of a radically other existence, the signs of a "barbarian language"—a language of suffering that he himself will come to speak during his own torture (121)—at the heart of civilization, signs that throw his humanist faith in civilization, his self-certainty, into crisis and turn him into an exemplary subject of doubt. The Magistrate's crisis of consciousness/conscience is ultimately a crisis of knowledge: although his mind is now radically opened up to the existence of otherness, this existence still remains inaccessible to him, as if the barbarian girl's experience has *encrypted* itself within his memory.

In an attempt to draw closer to the barbarian girl's experience, he engages her in acts of intimacy that only serve to emphasize their estrangement. Just as Susan "lose[s] the direction of [her] life" (30) in her attachment to Friday, the Magistrate's attachment to the barbarian girl causes him to "los[e] [his] way like a storyteller losing the thread of his story" (45). The Magistrate takes the girl into his bed, but rather than attempting to penetrate and thus "possess" her, he instead becomes absorbed in washing the surface of her body. These obscure meanderings of the Magistrate's desire make it explicit that we are working through the Magistrate's own grief as much as the barbarian girl's. Like Benjamin's Angel, the Magistrate would like to make whole what has been smashed. [30] His ritualistic washing of her body indicates an inability to work through his failure to put her body back together, an inability to absolve himself of having allowed the torture to take place in the first place. Like Lady Macbeth, he is unable to wash away the marks of his complicity.

Most critics have emphasized the ethically dubious nature of the Magistrate's caresses, quoting the passages in which he himself describes his actions as an ineffectual version of the Colonel's own ministrations. However, if we read his actions as an attempt to come to terms with "the impact of the torture chamber" on his life, then it becomes clear that the Magistrate's seemingly distanced self-absorption is at the same time an attempt to deal with his newfound awareness of the unbearable proximity of other lives. Although he claims that "if a change in my moral being were occurring, I would feel it," it is precisely this displacement of his own feelings that indicates an ethical change is indeed taking place: "I am the same man I always was; but time has broken, something has fallen in upon me from the sky, from nowhere: this body in my bed, for which I am responsible, or so it seems, otherwise why do I keep it?" (43). He kneels, then, at the feet of one who has fallen from the parallel realm, the "second sphere" (112), of the torture chamber. His posture suggests the sacred nature of our responsibility to the other. The Magistrate's revelation of his ethical relation to the other is a religious experience, an experience, in Emmanuel Levinas's terms, of the other as the incarnation of God.

Or in terms of Derrida's "hauntology," heavily indebted to Levinas's thought, the barbarian girl haunts the Magistrate's self-presence; her "return" is experienced by the Magistrate as a radical spatiotemporal dislocation, a "disjuncture" that announces "the very possibility of the other" (*Specters* 22). It is precisely when the *revenant* throws time and space "out of joint" that one is able to establish an ethical relation to that which haunts the present, to the suffering that underwrites history. However, if the Magistrate's consciousness is radically opened up to the fact of the barbarian girl's existence, her consciousness nevertheless remains closed off, inaccessible. Although he takes her into his bed, she remains cryptically other; although her life has invaded his, he is unable, unlike Colonel Joll, to make a significant impact on hers.

As a repetition of his traumatic awakening to the fact of the other's suffering, the Magistrate's caresses, like K's cultivation of his pumpkins, hover undecidably between a "healthy" process of working through and an "unhealthy" compulsion to repeat, between mourning and melancholia. Most of the "sessions" between the Magistrate and the girl end up with the Magistrate losing consciousness. "I lose myself in the rhythm of what I am doing. I lose awareness of the girl herself. There is a space of time which is blank to me: perhaps I am not even present" (28). He loses himself within the "rhythm," the repetitious nature, of his actions, returning to the very state of "oblivion" that has triggered off his *crise de conscience* in the first place: it is as if his mind is attempting to remember its initial attempt to remain oblivious to the cries coming from the granary. My explanation repeats the Magistrate's own confusion, for the true "desire" of this involuntary return is not clear at this point; it remains obscure as to whether the Magistrate's mind returns in order to remember or to forget, to hear the voices more clearly or to shut them out more completely. As Coetzee argues in "Confession and Double Thoughts" (*Doubling the Point* 251–95), one's innermost desires or motives must necessarily remain obscure.

Insofar as his bouts of oblivion cause him to forget himself and the girl, they are clearly the symptom of a desire to forget. However, insofar as his blackouts are gradually superseded by his dreams, they are also involved in a work of remembrance. In these dreams, both he and the girl take up the question of reparation. While the Magistrate renews his waking desire to repair the girl's body, to remember what the girl looked like before her mutilation, the girl herself constructs a model of the fort out of snow, out of the very substance of the Magistrate's forgetting: the snow of his dreams metonymically recalls the sand of the desert, but while the sand "perhaps buries the ruins of another fort" (15), the snow—with the aid of the girl—bodies it forth. The barbarian girl constructs a topographical model of the place where she lost her sight, a gesture of (dis)placement that serves only to underline her melancholia, her inability—at least in the Magistrate's dreams—to move beyond the site of her own loss.

However, the model fort also functions as a coded message, as the first of two secret gifts that the Magistrate receives from the girl. After the Magistrate has taken the girl back to her people and is subsequently himself locked up in the granary, it as if he has indeed—as the Colonel suspects—been in secret communication with the enemy. Like Friday's scattering of the petals, the construction of the fort is a mute indication of the place where her history went down, providing the Magistrate with a topographical map of her pain, one that will eventually allow him to navigate his own experience of torture.

The Magistrate is only able to receive the barbarian girl's "transmissions" once he has replaced his obscure desire *for* her with a seemingly perverse desire *to be* her. Just as Susan submits to Cruso's desire, the Magistrate seems almost wilfully to submit himself to Colonel Joll, as if in order to understand the barbarian girl's experience he must literally approximate it. This brings him closer to her not only because he physically experiences what she has experienced, but also because his torture seems to be a mode of penance for his attempt to remain oblivious to her suffering, a way of working through his singular responsibility for her suffering. Beyond his guilt as Magistrate, he is also guilty as an individual, as someone of finite resources who can never respond adequately to the fact that "somewhere, always, a child is being beaten." As we shall see, the Magistrate eventually acknowledges the monstrous proportions of this responsibility in "donating" to the barbarian girl the ultimate gift of his own (mock-)crucifixion, in "tak[ing] his own death upon himself" (Derrida, *The Gift of Death* 44).[31]

Having endlessly stared at the marks on the walls of his cell, seemingly no closer to deciphering these marks than he was to deciphering the marks on the girl's body, the Magistrate falls into a dream in which he is once more confronted with her body, or more specifically, with her feet: "The feet stand before me in the dust, disembodied, monstrous, two shapeless fish, two huge potatoes" (87). He picks up the feet, and subsequently the girl, and carries her across the yard, which now stretches "endless as the desert:" "There is no hope of reaching the other side, but I plod on, carrying the girl, *the only key I have to the labyrinth,* her head nodding against my shoulder, her dead feet drooping on the other side" (87; emphasis added). In his waking life, he then secures the key to a cellar, which, he happens to know, is also the key to the granary. The Magistrate attributes his intricate knowledge of the fort to "thirty years immersed in the minutiae of the life of the settlement" (90). However, his dream life would suggest that it is the barbarian girl's more intimate knowledge of what goes on in the fort that is the true key to the Magistrate's liberation.

The ethical argument of the novel depends on what use the Magistrate makes of this gift, on whether he can transform a temporary physical liberation into a more permanent form of emancipation. On his first escape from the granary, the Magistrate does not know what to do with his freedom, besides reinflicting on himself a form of torture or unfreedom in which he conceals himself under his former prostitute's bed while she makes love to a more youthful version of himself. This escape ends with him begging his guard to be readmitted into his cell. The second time around, his direction or duty is much clearer to him, as he attempts to halt a scene of *public* torture. This is the pivotal moment in the novel when torture is no longer concealed from sight, the moment when the Magistrate unlocks the door to the granary and attempts to make the people truly aware of what they are seeing. For, although the torture scene is now a public spectacle, its true nature remains hidden as long as the prisoners are seen as less than fully human. To put things another way, as Colonel Joll writes the word *enemy* on the prisoners' backs, torture is revealed as the erasure of the humanity of the tortured, a pedagogical spectacle that the Magistrate attempts to interrupt by making his own appeal to sight: "'Look!' I shout. 'We are the great miracle of creation. [. . .] Words fail me. 'Look at these men!' I recommence. 'Men!'" (107). Although his own vision is temporarily eclipsed by the blow he subsequently receives to the face, and although he has only momentarily succeeded in diverting the gaze of the crowd, he has succeeded in interrupting Joll's lesson in blindness. In common with protests against other forms of dehumanization, the Magistrate's words (the words of a man whose comfortable former life was dependent precisely on his capacity to remain oblivious) carry the ethical weight of an injunction: *Never forget!*

Critics—and especially his interviewers—have had problems locating Coetzee's own value system, in particular his relation to the liberal humanism that he sometimes seems to be satirizing in the various narratorial personae that he adopts. As the above passage makes abundantly clear, the language of humanism—with its fundamental belief in the dignity of man—remains the only possible language to protest acts of dehumanization. However, this language *returns* to the Magistrate in the wake of his recognition of the barbarous nature of civilization; it stutters and stumbles, no longer certain of itself:

> What after all do I stand for besides an archaic code of gentlemanly behaviour towards captures foes. . . . Would I have dared to face the crowd to demand justice for these ridiculous barbarians with their backsides in the air? Justice: once that word is uttered, where will it all end? . . . For where can that argument lead but to laying down our arms and opening the gates of the town to the people whose lands we have raped? (108)

His self-doubt, or rather his awareness of the unjust foundation of the civilized self, means that he is something like a posthumanist humanist, an agonistic position that the novel nonetheless presents as the only tenable ethical position available.

Validation of the Magistrate's actions comes in the form of a dream. After his protest, lying in agony on his cell floor, the Magistrate loses consciousness once more and is visited by the girl, dressed as a priestess, perhaps even as the Virgin Mary, in a dark blue robe and a cap embroidered with gold. Instead of another snow fort, she is building an oven. She offers him a "shapeless lump"—reminiscent of her disembodied feet in the last dream—which then changes into a loaf of bread with "a coarse, steaming, broken crust" (109). Even more explicitly than the food K cultivates in the desert, this is the bread of remembrance, eaten in remembrance of another scene of torture and as a promise of salvation. As Dick Penner puts it, her "gesture is as suggestive of a sacrament as his washing and oiling of her feet" (40). But what is perhaps less clear is that the Magistrate is receiving the sacrament of his *own* body: the wound on his face will later form a "crust like a fat caterpillar" (115) underlining its status as gift or stigma, as a sign of his own impending martyrdom.

However, this religious subtext remains just that, a sign system that remains confined to the Magistrate's dreams, a promise of redemption that remains closed off from the antiredemptive language of the narrative proper. I have emphasized the anti-idealist tradition in which I see Coetzee as writing precisely because his novels refuse to transcend history and the material world. This is perhaps most evident in the scenes of torture that follow from the Magistrate's dream of salvation in which he learns "what it meant to live in a body, as a body, a body which can entertain notions of justice only as long as it is whole and well, which very soon forgets them when its head is gripped and a pipe is pushed down its gullet and pints of salt water are poured into it till it coughs and retches and voids itself" (115). Such lessons in "the meaning of humanity" constitute an insistence on the materiality of the body, a moment of what one might call "negative transcendence," a descent that, like the final descent in *Foe*, brings the self into an abject, bodily relation with itself. In his dreams, the Magistrate's experience of torture brings him close to the barbarian girl—ultimately allowing him a form of access not only to her own experience of the "unfreedom" of torture but also to the potential freedom of her life outside of civilization. But at the same time the "waking" narrative resists this movement. His "lessons in the meaning of humanity" are really anti-lessons that leave him none the wiser in their reduction of knowledge to the "revelation" that "pain is truth; all else is subject to doubt" (5).

The Magistrate's "crucifixion" is a "spectacle of abasement" (120) in which, dressed in a woman's nightgown, he is hung first by his neck and then by his arms. At precisely the most extreme moment of physical suffering, he is granted a momentary glimpse of freedom. As the rope tightens around his neck, he loses consciousness and returns to his encounter with the barbarians in the foothills, one of whom is about to speak. On returning to consciousness, he is made to produce bellows of pain that a bystander recognizes as "barbarian language" (121). In an interview, Coetzee is asked whether the Magistrate is presented with "a sort of transcendent choice where [he] as it were go[es] over the edge into something new" ("Interview" 7). Coetzee replies by speaking of the choice "between the police and the empire and what they stand for, and the barbarian way of life," a choice that remains hypothetical since the Magistrate, too set in the ways of civilization, "cannot choose the barbarian way of life, although he makes vague gestures in that direction." The world-weary Magistrate (unlike the "childlike" Michael K), is unable to gain more than glimpses of a beyond to civilization, of an existence "outside the history that Empire imposes on its subjects" (154).

Nevertheless, the novel contains its own "chips of Messianic time" (Benjamin 263). In the interview, Coetzee goes on to suggest that "there is a very strong presence of children in the novel. . . . They might be able to make choices that [the Magistrate] finds impossible" (7). This presence of children is strongest at the end of the novel, when the Magistrate comes across some children building a snowman in the square (155). The scene brings a measure of psychological closure, in its exteriorization—or indeed exorcism—of the Magistrate's dreams. While the dreams began as a futile attempt to reconstruct, and to make reparations for, the past, the children's work, which makes the Magistrate feel "inexplicably joyful," is emphatically directed toward the future. However, the narrative ends with an explicitly anti-redemptive reminder of the gap separating dreams from reality: "This is not the scene I dreamed of. I leave it feeling stupid, like a man who lost his way long ago but presses on along a road that may lead nowhere" (156).[32]

INTIMATIONS OF FREEDOM

Although Coetzee's narratives rigorously resist the teleology of redemption, they are secretly directed toward the future. This secret leaning is most clearly evident in the characters' dream lives, as if something in their memories cannot quite give up the idea of freedom, as if they are waiting, like K, for what will begin once history, in all its repetitious "progress," has ended. In their waking, conscious lives, Coetzee's characters manifestly fail to make any headway; in their dreams—and it is no coincidence that all three narratives culminate in reverie—they seem, by contrast, to arrive at a kind of ethical understanding, a highly qualified *rapprochement* with the other.

The gap between privileged narrator and oppressed other is perhaps at its narrowest in *Waiting for the Barbarians*. Of all the narrators, it is the Magistrate who comes closest, thanks to Colonel Joll, to experiencing himself as other. And it is in the Magistrate's dreams that Coetzee comes closest to acknowledging the sacred dimensions of what it means to bear witness. In *Foe*,

Susan remains no closer to Friday than at the beginning of the narrative and Foe's theory about the ethical function of dreams as an encounter with "other phantoms" remains a theory that is only ambiguously put into practice in the novel's final descent. In *Life and Times of Michael K* the doctor is similarly unable to fathom the secret of Michael K's existence. However, because the doctor's viewpoint is supplemented by an indirect third person narration, we are able to follow Michael K out into the Karoo and gain a glimpse of what it would mean to exist outside the time of empire. Michael K's minimalist demonstration of how "one can live" is perhaps the most unequivocally affirmative of Coetzee's endings. In examining the novels in reverse order I have obviously not been able to trace the development of Coetzee's thinking during the years of the Emergency. I have nevertheless attempted to replicate the structure of the novels themselves, each of which ends with an intimation of what might lie beyond the impasse of apartheid.

What are we to make of these intimations? In "Remembering, Repeating and Working Through," Freud notes that "the patient does not remember anything that has been forgotten and repressed but acts it out. He reproduces it not as a memory but as an action. He repeats it, without, of course, knowing that he is repeating it" (147). The work of analysis, the process of working through, is the attempt to bring this history of repetition to consciousness, to put an end to the process of unconscious repetition: this is the logic behind the so-called talking cure—and behind conventional mourning as the verbalization of loss. Coetzee's novels, following Adorno's injunction to remain speechless before history, explicitly resist this logic. And yet, in the space opened up by their silence, something is nonetheless being worked through: early on in *Waiting for the Barbarians,* the Magistrate, like Freud himself, comes to question the ability of language to recover a history: "perhaps whatever can be articulated is falsely put. . . . Or perhaps it is the case that only that which has not been articulated has to be lived through" (65). At first glance, this second formulation seems to echo Freud's early thesis that one is doomed to act out what one is unable to remember; however, on closer inspection it suggests that acting out *is* a process of remembrance, that the "true" process of working through is nonverbal, that Coetzee's narratives, in their refusal to provide a direct articulation of apartheid, nevertheless constitute a mode of living through it.

Rather than mimetically reproducing the historical content of apartheid, Coetzee's novels grapple with the material, bodily affect of that history. Whereas a realist account of apartheid would turn it into a digestible historical narrative, allowing us to mourn and move on, Coetzee's novels resist this process of verbalization and relentlessly force us to confront the brute, indigestible materiality of the suffering engendered by apartheid. Instead of banishing or exorcising history, Coetzee's novels are themselves banished;

falling away, they leave us with the terrible, irreconcilable sight of the abused body, stripped bare of the explanatory narratives of historical discourse.

During the course of the TRC hearings, it became apparent that, for many of the bereaved, closure was dependent not so much on the recovery of the narrative, on the explanations, excuses, confessions, and denials of those who had tortured and killed their loved ones, as on the recovery of the bodily remains. The disfigured bodies of Friday, Michael K, and the barbarian girl are offered not as consolatory substitutes for the lost bodies of apartheid, but rather as a sign of the author's solidarity with the inconsolable demand of the bereaved.

CHAPTER TWO

RITES OF COMMUNION

––––––––––––

Wilson Harris's Hosting of History

And this—as I see it—is also the role of the author within his
ancestral background: he is the complex ghost of his own landscape
of history or work. To put it another way, his poem or novel is
subsistence of memory.

—Wilson Harris, "Interior of the Novel"

"There is always a coming storm," said Len. "Some unexpected
bloody uprising or act of terror. . . . When I consume a portion of
the morsel cooking in the sun, I lift the storm into sacramental
alignment with humanity. I invite humanity to summon all its
resources of creative foresight and to punch a hole in the coming
storm. Thereby it may find a way through the storm. It may
diminish the well-nigh overwhelming proportions of the coming
storm. But also, in consuming a perpetual morsel, a savaged
morsel, a universal morsel, I am able to take you back, Leonardo—
within the parameters of eternity—to the year 1519."

—Wilson Harris, *Resurrection at Sorrow Hill*

Wilson Harris's prolific fictional output is best understood as a repeated rite
of memorialization. Inviting us to consume the past as sacrament or "universal morsel," his work leads us to acknowledge our implication in the violence
and oppression that constitute the history of modernity. His work strives to
bring into being a new "corpus of sensibility" ("History, Fable and Myth" 27),

a sense of community in which individuals are bound together not by a common cultural inheritance but by a collective experience of loss and by a shared sense of responsibility for this loss. Like Glissant, he seeks to make the "void" of Caribbean history the basis for a new cross-cultural humanism. In place of the subject-centered politics of reclamation that characterize so many theories of multiculturalism, Harris offers us an other-orientated politics—and poetics—of relation. Instead of reclaiming a cultural heritage in order to (re)construct a particular version of Caribbean identity, Harris's hosting of history unhinges the identity of the subject in an attempt to bear witness to the spectral presence of that which colonialism has rendered "immaterial."

My epigraphs suggest two of the ways in which this hosting of history takes place, two of the ways in which Harris's work negotiates its relation to the immaterial. Harris's description of himself as "the complex ghost of his own landscape of history or work" indicates his desire to distance himself from the canonical conception of the author as sovereign subject, as the sole origin and guarantor of the work's meaning. For Harris, writing is the process of allowing one's individual personality or "bias" to be absorbed into the imaginative "landscape" of the work, a landscape that is itself drawn directly from the cultural history that forms the writer's "ancestral background." As the host organism, the writer is "consumed" by that which he creates. This idiosyncratic version of the death of the author includes the possibility of an authorial "afterlife" as the spirit or specter of his own work. Harris's relation to his work thus comes to parallel that of his ancestors to the present: in aligning himself with that which haunts "his own landscape of history," he too becomes "immaterial." His own spectrality or lack of substance becomes a way of remembering—bearing witness to—the absent presence of his ancestors.

But Harris also hosts history by rendering the immaterial material, by transforming history into the sacramental Host. In my second epigraph, the "morsel cooking in the sun" is the corpse of a child revolutionary in whose death Len—the schizophrenic double of Leonardo da Vinci and thus the representative of technological modernity—feels implicated. Len's consumption of this morsel parallels a number of religious rites of remembrance: the Carib practice of consuming a ritual morsel of a slain enemy and then fashioning a flute out of the bones, the Homeric *nekuia*, in which Odysseus slaughters a lamb and a ewe and invites the dead to come and drink of the blood, and, of course, the Christian Eucharist. In all three rituals, spirit becomes matter, and in consuming this sacred matter, the living become invested with the spirit of the dead. In the Carib ritual, the participants digest the enemy's secrets along with his flesh and then give voice to his spirit by playing the bone flute ("A Note on the Genesis of The Guyana Quartet" 9). In the *nekuia*, the sacrificial blood lends dead spirits substance and definition and enables Tiresias to voice the will of the gods. And in the Eucharist, the communicants become one with Christ's spirit by consuming His body and blood.

All three rites of remembrance are acts of homage and piety, recognitions of responsibility for the past that are also directed toward the future: Caribs hope to appease the spirit of the slain; Odysseus, condemned to wander the seas after blinding Poseidon's son, Polyphemos, is rewarded for his act of piety with the prophecy that he will eventually be allowed to return home to Ithaca; and Christians acknowledge their complicity in the death of Christ in the hope of salvation. Harris's own invocation or conjuration of the dead is also directed toward both the past and the future, and seeks to secure a similar promise or prophecy of redemption. Like Odysseus, he pays homage to the spirits of the past in order "to find a way through the coming storm" (*Resurrection at Sorrow Hill*, 137).

These two modes of hosting history ultimately converge into one activity. On the one hand, to host history is to pacify the authorial subject, to literalize the model of the generous, self-effacing host who, like Christ at the Last Supper, invites his guests to participate in his own consumption. On the other, to host history is to activate the object, to give life or voice to the dead. Whereas literary acts of witnessing and testimony are often associated with realist narratives narrated by those who have undergone a particular historical event—as in the Latin American genre of the *testimonio*—Harris's hosting of history implies a relinquishing of his own experience and a taking on of the experience of others. The activity of narration thus becomes a mode of suffering, not just the recounting of an event but an event in itself, the site of a transformation of history. For Harris, to bear witness (a verb that is itself caught between activity and passivity) to history is to redeem it.[1] Inspired by T. S. Eliot's use of Tiresias in *The Waste Land*, Harris repeatedly adopts (and adapts) the persona of the Greek seer. By taking up the empathic position of someone who has "foresuffered all" (*The Waste Land* 243), Harris is able to invest the events he witnesses with religious significance. However, while Eliot recognizes pagan rituals merely as precursors to Christianity, Harris's less Eurocentric sense of history produces a more truly eclectic, cross-cultural sense of the sacred, one that refuses to confine itself to specific dogma or creed.

In Harris's work, the passionate activity of bearing witness mediates not only between spirit and matter, activity and passivity, subject and object, but also between the past and the future. To become "the ghost of [one's] own landscape of history or work" is to become the medium through which the dead come to articulate themselves, and make a difference in, the course of the lives of the living. To awaken the dead is to invite them to intercede in the destiny of the present, to offer humanity "the ghost of a chance" of redemption. This phrase recurs at critical disjunctures—moments when the past seems to return to interrupt the present time of the narrative—in all four of the novellas that make up *The Guyana Quartet*. In all but the first of these novellas, the spirit of the dispossessed returns in order to offer the community of the living the chance to acknowledge their indebtedness. It returns as Oudin in *The Far Journey of Oudin*, the double of the murdered heir to a coastal plantation; as Cristo in *The Whole Armour*, who reemerges from the jungle bearing the coat of the mythical jaguar and the memory of "every black ancestor and bloodless ghost" in South America (343); and as Poseidon in *The Secret Ladder*, the ancient leader of a group of maroons (originally runaway slaves) who returns after his own death to avert further bloodshed, and to remind both his maroons and the surveying crew who plan to flood their land not only of "the ghost of responsibility" (463) but also of their responsibility toward ghosts. These three figures function as the sacrificial host, indeed as Christ himself: Oudin's status as the murdered heir to a plantation recalls Christ's parable of the tenants, in which the tenants of a vineyard murder the owner's son rather than pay their dues (Luke 20: 9–16). Cristo's name presages his own trial and death for crimes of which he is innocent. And the "secret ladder of conscience" to which Poseidon is "hooked and nailed" suggests a similar rite of crucifixion (371). Their deaths restage historical acts of murder and dispossession and thereby repoliticize the (pre-)Christian ritual by turning it into a mode of historical consciousness/conscience.

By contrast, in *Palace of the Peacock* it is the narrator or Dreamer who functions as "the ghost of a chance," returning to the world of the dead in order to replay a colonizing voyage upriver and offer the crew a chance of "changing [their] ways" (51). If the plot structure of the other novellas emphasizes the hosting or presencing of the immaterial, *Palace of the Peacock* emphasizes the spectral role of the author as the host imagination. By figuring the narrator, rather than a character internal to the narrative, as the redemptive spectral presence, Harris foregrounds both the role of the artist as "the complex ghost of his own landscape or work" and the act of narration as a creative repetition of history. His presence as witness is, I shall argue, the difference within the repetition, that which enables history to redeem itself.

In the sections that follow I distinguish Harris's hosting of history from the secular—or at least not explicitly religious—modes of mourning and bearing witness that were the focus of the last chapter, explore the philosophical and artistic models from which Harris derives his approach, examine two of Harris's essays on art as a mode of historical witness, and offer a reading of *Palace of the Peacock*. If, as many critics have noted, Harris's later work returns obsessively to this first breakthrough novel, it is because its emphasis on the act of narration anticipates the metafictional orientation of his later work. While the basic mythic plot structure of sacrifice and redemption remains the same throughout Harris's oeuvre, it is the act of narration itself that becomes the focus of his novelistic energies, lending each repetition its (re)creative difference. The proliferation of narratorial personae that characterizes Harris's later work thus becomes a testament to his generosity as host, to the endlessness of his desire to bear witness to history.

A Sacred Art in a Secular World

Harris's work renders explicit the sacred dimensions of the work of mourning that remain implicit in Coetzee's fiction. I placed Coetzee's work alongside that of Derrida and Adorno because all three are fundamentally secular—as much post-Holocaust as post-Enlightenment thinkers. Adorno's dictum concerning the barbarity of poetry after Auschwitz can be read as a statement about the absolute loss of faith demanded by the Holocaust, a loss of faith that would seem to render poetry an impossibility—even, one might say, a blasphemy—insofar as poetry (or any other art form) is an act of faith. If art is to survive Auschwitz, then its status as an act of faith—in either the human or the divine—must remain a secret. Harris's explicit sacralization of history is precisely what most post-Holocaust writers have resisted; indeed the word *Holocaust* itself has been abandoned by many writers precisely because of its sacrificial overtones.[2] If a post-Holocaust work of art contains intimations of redemption, then these intimations must remain buried within the work, like the cryptic dreams of the Magistrate in *Waiting for the Barbarians*.

In Harris's fiction these dreams of redemption are, by contrast, constitutive of the work itself. There is no definitive break between the waking and dream lives of the characters; the work itself is a dream work. Harris's novels thus seem—at least from a European perspective—peculiarly anachronistic or nonmodern. This is not because Harris dismisses the significance of the Holocaust, nor simply because he places it within a wider history of genocide, colonization, and destruction. Rather, Harris is *deliberately* anachronistic: he conceives of his art as an act of faith fully aware that history itself provides no such ground for the maintenance of faith. To put it another way, it is precisely his awareness of contemporary crisis, his sense of history as catastrophe, that leads him to argue the importance of an art of redemption.

At the beginning of one of his later novels, *Resurrection at Sorrow Hill*, which usefully presents itself as a meta-commentary on the whole of Harris's oeuvre, Harris has his narrator dramatize and defend his narration as an act of faith. Although—or rather precisely because—he recognizes that the community under Sorrow Hill exists "virtually . . . without a future," he sees it as the artist's role to "visualize the Shadow of resurrection . . . as a numinous embodiment of potential creativity in the community" (9):

I did not deceive myself. I knew how disadvantaged the people were. And
yet in my dreams it was as if Daemon had sculpted the poor world under
Sorrow Hill into a staff upon which the creative genius of space leaned
for support. Impossible, some would say. (9–10)

Harris thus presents his fiction not as escapist fantasy but as a mode of con-
fronting the sorry state of the world (hence *Sorrow* Hill) that nevertheless
affirms the potential for recreation (in both senses of the word). Daemon, who
is thrown into a state of melancholic despair by the drowning of his pregnant
wife, must be taught how to "play" with history. Later on in the novel, Len's
"telescopic memory" is able to retrieve an image of Daemon's wife and child
from "the rapids of history" (135). The explicit aim of Len's "Sorrow Hill cin-
ema" (135), and of the restaging of history that takes place throughout the
novel, is not so much to deny that which has taken place as to bring about an
alteration of perspective, to cure Daemon of his despair by making him see
history *differently,* that is, transfigured by faith or Hope (the name of one of
the narrators). Harris's fiction thus attempts not so much to return to a pre-
Holocaust mode of remembrance as to move beyond our contemporary crisis
of remembrance: one might say that his art of memory is not so much sacred
as "post-secular."

     In the previous chapter, I noted how Rosemary Jolly employs Harris's
concept of a "frontier novel"[3] to suggest how Coetzee's allegories are "true to
the violent domain of conquest in the present . . . but . . . remain faithful to
the future in that its crucial locations are those which suggest the potential for
transition" (78). However, there is a crucial difference between Coetzee's secular allegories and Harris's mythic narratives: while Coetzee's narratives retain
a certain ideological proximity to the history that they allegorize, Harris's narratives explicitly attempt to break free of fixed ideological positions. As part
of his insistence on remaining "true to the violent domain of conquest," Coetzee scrupulously retains a sense of the gap separating the privileged and the
oppressed, the colonizer and the colonized. By contrast, Harris's exploration
of what he terms a "complex mutuality" ("Adversarial Contexts" 127) *enacts*
rather than merely "*suggest*[s] the potential for transition" (emphasis added).
While Coetzee's "negative image" of South African society eschews the
inessentials of time and place in order to throw the ideological constraints
governing apartheid and other systems of colonialism into relief, Harris's
mythic narratives erect a "Shadow constellation" in order to suggest a world of
alternative possibilities, a hidden dimension in which our modes of being and
relating are not entirely determined by history.

     This difference between an art that yearns for a transformation of history
and an art that enacts this transformation is the crucial difference between a
secular and a postsecular understanding of bearing witness. This difference of

perspective becomes evident in Hena Maes-Jelinek's comparison of Coetzee's *In the Heart of the Country* with Wilson Harris's *Carnival*. Her own distrust of what she sees as "postmodern scepticism"—leads Maes-Jelinek to valorize Harris's "dialogic" liberating vision and to lament what she sees as Coetzee's "monologic" and "tragically 'blocked muse'" (92).[4] Both novels attempt to establish a dialogue between the narrator and "an other outside the self with whom a dialogue must be established in order to create a saving plurivocity" (90). However, while Coetzee's narrator remains trapped within the prison house of her self-reflexive monologue, unable to establish "words of true exchange" (Coetzee 101) between herself and her black servants on a South African farm, Harris's narrator discovers that he "contains many others within himself, guides who lead him into the labyrinth of history" (Maes-Jelinek 91).

Echoing, oddly enough, the neo-Marxist critique of Coetzee, Maes-Jelinek takes Magda's inability to establish a dialogue as evidence of Coetzee's "shrinking away from a genuine exploration of history" (91). It should be clear from chapter 1 that this failure to establish a dialogue is in fact a precise fidelity to the historical conditions under which the novel was written and that the novel protests: the stones that Magda arranges on the hillside at the end of the novel are desperate attempts to communicate, offerings placed in memory of the hope of an end to apartheid. It would be easy enough to reverse the terms of Maes-Jelinek's critique and argue that it is, in fact, Harris's mythic narratives that reveal "a shrinking away from a genuine exploration of history," that Harris's vision of redemption renders his novels ahistorical fantasy. It becomes necessary here to determine the exact nature of the relation between Harris's texts and history, between the artist and the world—to establish the nature of what critics have variously understood as Harris's "dialectical imagination."

A degree of critical confusion reigns over the exact nature of Harris's dialectic—if it is indeed a dialectic. Many critics see Harris's work in terms of the union of contraries, a model Michael Gilkes traces back to Harris's interest in medieval alchemy and Jungian archetypes. Both theories suggest a marriage of preconstituted, and thus undialectical, terms. Because neither theory accounts for the subject's relation to the world or to history, the unfortunate effect of Gilkes's otherwise sensitive analysis is to reduce Harris's narratives to a static, ahistorical formula.

In another book-length study of Harris's work, Sandra Drake relates Harris's project to deconstruction. Derrida's recent emphasis on the ethical importance of recognizing one's debt to the "not-present" is certainly close to Harris's emphasis on the importance of bearing witness to the "immaterial," and during the course of this chapter I shall attempt to highlight some of the places where their projects—in particular their thoughts concerning spectrality and mourning—appear to converge. However, while there are many similarities between the two writers, I would have to agree with Maes-Jelinek that their projects are ultimately divergent. This is not, as Maes-Jelinek claims (in my view, mistakenly), because Derrida tends to "fall back on the text or on language as the only reality" ("Ambivalent Clio" 96), but because there is a crucial difference between Derrida's desire to develop a mode of bearing witness to history that is free from "metaphysico-religious determination" (*Specters of Marx* 89) and Harris's explicitly sacred or postsecular understanding of bearing witness. Drake's failure to register this difference leads to an uneasy avoidance of the spiritual aspect of Harris's work, to the highly unconvincing argument that *Palace of the Peacock,* for instance, "is not really a tale of either salvation or redemption" (68).

Jeremy Poynting and Gregory Shaw, by contrast, are all too aware of what they describe as Harris's "metaphysics." Poynting argues that "far from showing the spiritual and material in necessary interpenetration, the radical import of *[The Far Journey of Oudin]* is frequently undermined by its metaphysical idealism" (126). Alerted to the fact that Harris was "never without several volumes of Hegel" (Shaw 147) during his time in the Guyanese interior, Shaw argues that Harris's fiction constitutes a "drive toward abstraction" (142) that operates according to a Hegelian dialectic in which the material is progressively overcome, even conquered, by the progress of World Spirit. Shaw's description of Harris's use of language is a fine one:

> The Harrisian word, the Harrisian image, tend to possess a peculiarly dialectical quality of negating themselves. . . . The impression is of a reduction or subtilising of matter to its most extreme or visionary form, matter stretched or attenuated to breaking point, dissolved or atomised, as it were. . . . Images crumble, shift, dissolve and coalesce in strange combinations . . . reflecting a universe in the process of becoming. (147)

Although this is an accurate microdescription of what happens at one level of Harris's work, Shaw's analysis is less persuasive in its argument concerning the overall purpose of this attenuation of matter. For Shaw, the ultimate consequence of Harris's dialectic is a narcissistic absorption of the world into the consciousness of the artist: "Just as in Hegel the quest of spirit culminates in the absolute consciousness of the philosopher, so in the typical Harris novel the hero's quest culminates in the apotheosis of the artist who is the embodiment of that self-same spirit" (148). Shaw's reading of Harris thus parallels the Marxist reading of Hegel as an idealist, which ignores the lengths to which Hegel goes to establish the immanent nature of his dialectic. What Shaw sees as the apotheosis of the artist might equally well be described as the sublation of the artist within his material. When Harris describes himself as the ghost of his own work he may well have in mind Hegel's anti-idealist conception of spirit: "This spirit is consciousness but it is also the object of consciousness . . . this then is how the spirit acquires a content; it does not find a content outside itself, but makes itself its own object and content" (47).

However, Harris's political concern for that which modernity considers "immaterial," for that which has been violently erased or forgotten in the name of historical progress, is emphatically *un*Hegelian. Andrew Benjamin's argument that Harris's texts enact a Nietzschean process of becoming is altogether more persuasive, not least because Nietzsche developed his thought of eternal return in explicit opposition to Hegel's idea of dialectical progression, which, he argued, "transforms every moment into a naked admiration for success" ("On the Uses and Disadvantages of History for Life" 105). For Benjamin, the Harrisian narrative enacts the perpetual becoming of history by "crumbling" the static, continuous time in which history is usually conceived. What Shaw sees as Harris's "subtilising of matter" may in fact be closer to Nietzsche's destruction of appearance. Andrew Benjamin's argument is a short but dense reading of a passage from one of Harris's less well-known novellas, *The Eye of the Scarecrow*. His argument exists in a critical vacuum insofar as he makes no reference to other critics and their interpretations of Harris's "dialectic," and insofar as no other critics make reference to his argument. My discussion seeks to extend Benjamin's insights by relating Nietzsche's thought of eternal return to his earlier idea of critical history and by relating both to the process of hosting history that characterizes Harris's entire oeuvre.

Harris's hosting of history is not so much a resolution of the subject-object split as a refusal of the distinction between the two. Whereas Hegel's concept of dialectical progression is, at least in the first instance, a rational positing of the world as the object of contemplation, Nietzsche's thought of eternal return is not so much a concept—grounded in rational logic—as an intuition or experience. Eternal return is not a thought *about* existence but a thought that itself transforms existence. For Nietzsche, the artist's relation to the world is exemplary of this nonrational thought because art is an experiencing, rather than a contemplation, of life. The "complex mutuality" that I have attempted to evoke in my description of Harris's work as a hosting of history is also suggested by Nietzsche's description of "the world as a work of art that attempts to give birth to itself" (*The Will to Power* 796, qtd. in Stambaugh 82). Art, for Nietzsche, is an experience that the artist and the world mutually undergo: "man becomes the transfigurer of existence when he learns to transfigure himself" (*The Will to Power* 820, qtd. in Stambaugh 82). Although Nietzsche is often thought of as the harbinger of postmodern scepticism and even—erroneously—of nihilism, his view of art as the "transfiguration and affirmation of human existence" (Stambaugh 82) is in stark contrast to Adorno's post-Holocaust aesthetics and the muted, negative affirmation of Beckett or Coetzee.

Benjamin argues that Harris's artistic practice of infinite rehearsal, like Nietzsche's thought of eternal return, constitutes a transvaluation of history that attempts to move beyond both redemptive nostalgia and the nihilism of historical determinism. Bearing in mind my emphasis on the sacred dimensions of Harris's understanding of bearing witness, one might be tempted to argue that Harris's work falls back into a mode of redemptive nostalgia. However, Nietzsche's polemic is directed against the Christian nostalgia for a "back-world." For Nietzsche, Christianity is itself a form of nihilism in that its valorization of heaven inevitably betrays a contempt for the world, a desire to escape the burden of existence. Harris's polemic against what he sees as postmodern nihilism, like Nietzsche's polemic against the Christian doctrine of *contemptus mundi*, is motivated by the same desire to affirm the possibility of transformation in this world rather than the next.

To see Harris's work as an affirmation of existence that moves beyond both Christianity and nihilism is to gain an insight into its anachronistic—or to use Nietzsche's word, untimely—impact. It is precisely this sense of Harris's untimeliness that is missing from Paul Sharrad's "The Art of Memory and the Liberation of History: Wilson Harris's Witnessing of Time." Sharrad argues that Harris's conception of his art as a mode of witnessing history is indebted to his interest in the medieval *ars memoria*, and specifically to the memory plays of Giulio Camillo, which endlessly recombined units of memory in order to arrive at a picture of "the whole of history remembered from above, as it were" (Yates 212, qtd. in Sharrad 117). To gain such a view of history would be to know the mind of God. However, by exclusively emphasizing Harris's debt to the *ars memoria*, Sharrad neglects to approach the problem of Harris's contemporaneity: What does it mean to witness history "from above" in a secular age?[5] How might a medieval worldview offer "a genuinely radical liberation for a post-colonial world" (124)? The radical import of Harris's witnessing of history only becomes clear if one sees his art as a postsecular, postnihilist mode of remembrance.[6]

In his essay "On the Uses and Disadvantages of History for Life," Nietzsche distinguishes among three modes of history that might be practiced in the interests of life: the monumental, the antiquarian, and the critical.[7] It is the last mode, which anticipates his later thought of eternal return, that seems to me to provide the clearest description of Harris's own project. "If he is to live," Nietzsche writes, "man must possess and from time to time employ the strength to break up and dissolve a part of the past" (75). Critical history wants to be "clear as to how unjust the existence of anything—a privilege, a cast, a dynasty—is, and how greatly this thing deserves to perish" (76). Like Harris's narratives, in which "one relives and reverses the given conditions of the past" ("Tradition" 36), critical history directs itself against historical determinism by constructing a *fantasy* past: "it is the attempt to give oneself, as it were *a posteriori*, a past in which one would like to originate in opposition to that in which one did originate" (76). Critical history is nothing less than the attempt to change human nature, the attempt "to confront our inherited nature with our knowledge and through a stern new discipline combat our inborn heritage and implant in ourselves a new habit, a new instinct, a second nature so that our first nature withers away" (76). Critical history is related to eternal return in that both modes of repetition are an attempt to recover what Nietzsche refers to as "the innocence of becoming" (Stambaugh 12). Harris's untimely recourse to myth is an attempt to recover a similarly radical innocence that would set us free from what he terms "the fixed conceptions" of our time.

It is possible to see Nietzsche's thought of eternal return as a prototype of Freud's principle of working through. In both cases, a qualified redemption—some sort of release from, or overcoming of, time—is achieved by becoming conscious of a cycle of repetition. Both theories offer a way out of helplessness, passivity, and determinism not by asserting the possibility of free will and autonomy but simply by recognizing the pattern of events in which one is caught. Nietzsche's insight that "the fact of consciousness itself alters the character of recurrence" (Stambaugh 34) is also Freud's. Both theories describe this coming-to-consciousness as a subjective, aesthetic experience rather than an objective, scientific deduction, as a revelation (Nietzsche likened his thought of eternal return to a dream or a prophecy) of the pattern into which history (either personal or collective) falls. Both Nietzsche's thought of eternal return and Harris's practice of infinite rehearsal are thus antidotes to the involuntary, passive, life-denying relation to time that is associated with melancholia, which, like Christianity, can lead to a loss of regard for the things of this world. The Tiresian practice of "foresuffering all" is transformed into carnival: the despairing, tragic figure of Tiresias in *The Waste Land* becomes the comedic grandmother of Hope in *Resurrection at Sorrow Hill*, a shaman in a " giant Arawak head-dress," "a creature of sublime (however absurd) masquerade" (6). Harris's novels might thus be described as a kind of cheerful or "gay" mourning, a mourning performed in the interests of life.[8]

Learning How to Inherit a Disinheritance

Cheerfulness is both the tenor and the ethic of Harris's essays on how the radical loss of culture engendered by slavery and colonialism might be transformed into the ground of a new cross-cultural sensibility. I want to pause to consider two of Harris's early essays, "History, Fable and Myth in the Caribbean and the Guianas" and "Interior of the Novel: Amerindian/African/European Relations," for what they have to say about the relationship between literature and collective trauma, a topic that has recently received a lot of critical attention.[9]

"History, Fable and Myth in the Caribbean and the Guianas," starts out by rejecting the teleological perspective of modernity that governs both James Froude's infamous assertion of the historyless, culturally impoverished state of the Caribbean and the attempt by his contemporary, J. J. Thomas, to rebut Froude's assertion. For Harris, both writers ignore the "primitive manifestations [of culture] which signified for them a 'relapse into obeahism, devil-worship and children eating'" (24). To Harris, these "primitive manifestations" are "the epic stratagems available to Caribbean man in the dilemmas of history which surround him," the creative resources that enable the Caribbean writer to bring into being a "Caribbean architecture of consciousness" (25).

Harris's argument here is not the conventional nationalist argument that the postcolonial writer is able to construct a sense of identity by drawing on an indigenous cultural tradition. For Harris, it is precisely the discontinuous nature of the Caribbean cultural inheritance—whether indigenous or imported—that enables the Caribbean writer to confront "the dilemmas of history that surround him" (25). In *Specters of Marx*, Derrida writes: "To bear witness would be to bear witness to what we are insofar as we inherit, and that—here is the circle, here is the chance or the finitude—we inherit the very thing that allows us to bear witness to it" (54). In other words, one's cultural inheritance provides the very means of bearing witness to it; one inherits that which allows one to pay one's debt to the past. But what happens if a community is deprived of its cultural inheritance, shorn of its ability to remember its own ancestors? This is the implicit question behind Harris's exploration of limbo dancing and the "possession trances" of Haitian *vodun*, rites of *dis*inheritance that bear witness not to the richness of Caribbean culture but to a *loss* of culture, to the historyless void of the Middle Passage. The movements of the limbo dancer physically recall the way in which "the slaves contorted themselves into human spiders" in the cramped conditions onboard the slave ships. Haitian and other forms of Caribbean *vodun* also bear witness to the dislocation of the Middle Passage precisely because, unlike African forms of *vodun*, they cannot make a direct appeal to the tribal ancestors (33). Both limbo and *vodun* are "gateways" not to an African cultural plenitude but to a collective experience of loss; they do not so much recover an African tradition as remember a severance from that tradition.

It would be tempting to link these rites to the bodily forms of remembrance enacted by Coetzee's figures of alterity and to see limbo and *vodun* as ways of remaining inconsolable, as radical refusals to forget the injustices of slavery. However, in Coetzee's work bodily rituals are closer to melancholia than to mourning because of Coetzee's reluctance to attribute a redemptive meaning to suffering. Because we do not have access to the interior lives of his figures of alterity, we cannot tell whether their silent rituals afford them relief. For Harris, by contrast, such rituals are unambiguously cathartic; they constitute "a profound art of *compensation* which seeks to replay a dis-memberment of the tribe . . . and to invoke at the same time a curious psychic reassembly of the parts of the dead muse and god" (28; emphasis added). Harris makes a cross-cultural virtue out of the way in which the slave trade deliberately dispersed members of the same tribe. While African *vodun* is "a school of ancestors," Haitian *vodun* "breaks the tribal monolith of the past and reassembles an inter-tribal or cross-cultural community of families" (33). Harris's interest in myths of dis-membering and re-membering a tribal god parallels Nietzsche's interest in Dionysus in *The Birth of Tragedy*. For both writers, such myths imply the possibility of a (re)creative destruction. This belief in the recreative power of art allows Harris to rewrite rituals of disjuncture and dispossession as cross-cultural bricolage, as the "renascence of a new corpus of sensibility [the pun draws attention to the physical process of re-membering or reincarnating the tribal god] that could translate and accommodate African and other legacies within a new architecture of cultures" (27).

In "Interior of the Novel: Amerindian/African/European Relations," the emphasis shifts from the pagan logic of re-membering the "corpus" to the Christian poetics of transubstantiation. The essay begins by exploring a "curious footnote" to the history of the colonization of Guyana. An Amerindian chief approaches an English governor to claim payment for "services his fighting forces had rendered to the occupying powers," hinting largely at the presence of these forces in the bush. The governor subsequently discovers that there are in fact no forces in the bush, that the chief possesses only "a nightmare relic." Harris's dense interpretation of this "displacement" is worth quoting in full:

> The Amerindian king has been unmasked as a shamanistic trickster (on one hand) while (on the other) the statecraft of the Governor draws him back, as it were, to discover a spectral host—a vanished people—part and parcel of a crucifixion of appetite, his and their appetite for adventure, their and his appetite for security. A new hunger—a new subsistence of memory—comes into play wherein both sovereign statecraft and primitive king are implicated in the dust of history blowing as it were towards a new terrifying yet immaterial conception: an art of fiction where the agents of time begin to subsist upon the real reverses the human spirit has endured, the real chasm of pain it has entered, rather than the apparent consolidation, victories and battles it has won. (13)

Harris's essays, like his novels, owe much to the associative logic of his imagery. The revelation of the tribe's absence is initially referred to as "one of those peculiar holes in the body of history" (11), holes he then describes as "stigmata of the void" (12). The reference to Christ's body is reinforced by the pun on "host" and by the dense expression, "crucifixion of appetite," with the result that it is as if the "spectral host" becomes the sacrament of which both king and governor partake. This metonymic displacement forces them both to acknowledge their guilty "appetite," their shared responsibility for the fate of the tribe, and then transforms this "appetite" into a "new hunger—a new subsistence of memory." Both the governor and the chief must learn to live in remembrance of the lost tribe. Crucially, this recognition of a mutual responsibility brings the two parties into a new relation with each other, as they are filled with an awareness of history as a "chasm of pain." The shift from the material to the immaterial is precisely not a movement toward abstraction; it is instead a materialization of that which has only just begun to matter, to make an impact on the consciousness/conscience of the living: not the tribe itself, but its absence. This materialization of the immaterial forces both the governor and the chief to become conscious of the tribe's extinction, forces them to become historically (self-)conscious. To relate to the tribe as "subsistence of memory"—a phrase that in itself seems to render the immaterial material—is both to learn how to live off, to draw life-giving sustenance from, the memory of the tribe (and its demise) and also to keep the memory of the tribe itself alive.

The passage is reminiscent of Walter Benjamin's "Theses on the Philosophy of History." Harris's attempt to bear witness to the immaterial is clearly linked to Benjamin's insistence on remembering the history of barbarity that underwrites the history of civilization. In the last chapter I related Benjamin's Angel of History to the project of both negative dialectics and deconstruction. However, the religious aspects of Benjamin's "mystical Marxism" are clearly a problem for these secular traditions. Although Benjamin's "Theses on the Philosophy of History" is central to Derrida's meditation on mourning and Marxism in *Specters of Marx,* his main analysis of them is limited to an agonistic footnote. Derrida would like to inherit the spirit of Benjamin's messianic promise while distinguishing this messianic spirit from "messianism" as such (180–81). Like Coetzee, Derrida would like to keep his dreams of redemption a secret.

The difference between a secular and a sacred or postsecular mode of remembrance is one of perspective. For both Derrida and Coetzee, it is not possible to transcend one's own historicity and view history "from above." Coetzee's narrators are scrupulously earth-bound, unable to transcend the ideological implications of their own subject-position. If they are to gain an insight into the historical "chasm of pain," they must, like the Magistrate, experience this pain first hand. And even then, this experience is only obscurely revelatory and may well leave one "feeling stupid" (*Waiting for the Barbarians* 156). By contrast, Harris gains his "overview" of history by transforming himself into "the ghost of his own landscape of history or work." And it is this gesture that relates his work to the philosophy of history. A view from above is the basic condition of a philosophy of history's possibility, insofar as "history" is inevitably constituted as the object of "philosophy." One might describe the philosophy of history as a succession of attempts to abdicate this transcendent position. Hegel's *Geist*, Nietzsche's *Übermensch* (for it is the *Übermensch* who attains to the vision of history as eternal return), and Benjamin's Angel are all products of their authors' attempts to immerse philosophy in the material. I want to pause for a moment to consider the nature of Benjamin's Angel's immersion, as an *image* of mourning that graphically illustrates—as a description of a sketch should—the nature of Harris's attempt to bear witness to history.

In order to view history as "one single catastrophe" (Benjamin 257), one needs to see things from the perspective of eternity, but in order to bear witness to this catastrophe, one needs to suffer as a mortal. As the incarnation of God's Spirit, angels mediate between the human and the divine; they announce God's sense of time to humans. While angels traditionally appear to forewarn humanity of what will come to pass, Benjamin's Angel comes to announce the past, to announce an event that has yet to happen both in and to the past. "Every second of time," Benjamin tells us, "was the strait gate through which the Messiah might enter." If there is a relation between Nietzsche, Benjamin, and their respective philosophies of history, it is in their mutual rejection of teleology, in their insistence that freedom is linked to repetition rather than progress.

However, Benjamin's warning that "even the dead will not be safe from the enemy if he wins" (255) does not simply mean that the true historical materialist seeks to bury the dead, for this would be a conservative mode of remembering in order to forget. To bear witness to history is rather to testify to the unburial of the dead, to the way in which the ongoing momentum of historical progress perpetually disallows the burial of its victims. Benjamin's Angel sees history as a process of desecration and his inability to bring about closure finds its physical correlative in the forced openness of his eyes, mouth, and wings: "His eyes are staring, his mouth is open, his wings are spread" (257). The act of seeing—witnessing in its most neutral sense—is here transformed first into grief at being able to do no more than witness, at not being able to bury the dead or "make whole what has been smashed," and thence into a bodily form of remembrance or *bearing* witness.

Benjamin's last work stands on a threshold between the secular and the sacred, not least in its uncanny presentiment of the Holocaust. While the authenticity of the Angel's grief is unambiguous, the significance of his suffering remains undecidable. For the post-Holocaust tradition in which I have located Coetzee's work, the Angel's witnessing remains an agonized, inconsolable recognition that every moment is in want of—waiting for—

redemption. For Harris, by contrast, the Angel's witnessing in itself constitutes a mode of redemption. While Harris believes in art's capacity to transfigure existence, Coetzee sees his art as "too slow, too old-fashioned, too
indirect to have any but the slightest and most belated effect on the life of
the community or the course of history" ("Jerusalem Prize Acceptance
Speech" 98–99). Indeed, he concludes his speech by updating and revising
Nietzsche's view of art: "We have art, said Nietzsche, so that we shall not die
of the truth. In South Africa, there is now too much truth for art to hold,
truth by the bucketful, truth that overwhelms and swamps every act of the
imagination" (99). For Harris, what he calls the subjective imagination is
still capable of "overwhelming" the truth of history, of triumphing over
nihilism. Nevertheless, it is important not to overemphasize the difference
between these two positions: Coetzee is unable to avoid the hope that his
vigil might one day make a difference, while Harris must finally acknowledge that his art can only run "*in parallel with* all wasted lives waiting to be
redeemed" (*Carnival* 167; emphasis added).

In the second half of "Interior of the Novel," Harris moves on to explain
why the novel must go beyond realism in order to bear witness to the absent
body of the tribe. The disappearance of the tribe—which presumably took
place over a number of decades (the chief wants the governor to recognize an
agreement that precedes British rule in Guyana)—is only an event that begins
to become historical—begins to "matter"—when the chief inadvertently
draws the governor's attention to the absence of his tribe. The tribe only figures in the historical record as a "fictitious presence" (14). The realist novel is
incapable of registering this presence as anything other than a fiction because
realism relies on a distinction between the actual and the imaginary. To
"recover" the tribe's history would be to endow it with a presence that it never
actually had in history. Thus Harris calls for a new form of fiction that is capable of registering the "absent presence" of the tribe.

Such a fiction would have to reject "the sovereign individual as such"
precisely because slavery and colonization constituted the denial of individual
agency and humanity. In order to bear witness to this denial, the novel needs
to abandon its moorings within the individual consciousness:

> Where [Georg] Lukács speaks of a 'middle-of-the-road' hero within his
> besieged marxist premises I must speak of a middle-of-the-landscape
> sculpture or waterfall or river or escarpment of jungle or rockface down
> which a phenomenal erosion happened, quite suddenly, precipitately, of
> conquered peoples. The Ibo of Nigeria are a terrifying example of the
> engulfment which can suddenly overtake a people within a trauma of
> helplessness—external conquest, internal collapse. There is a reason to
> believe that the earliest forms of tragic art were born out of a necessity to
> compensate such losses within the human psyche. (16)

Harris's description recalls both Benjamin's description of the crisis of storytelling produced by World War I and the cataclysmic onset of modernity and Freud's analysis of trauma as an event so overwhelming that it is not possible to be (mentally) present at the time of its occurrence, as an event that can only be belatedly witnessed. Harris here suggests that colonization may produce a similar kind of trauma, precisely because it disrupts the colonized culture's frame of reference. Although the colonization of the Ibo, like the disappearance of the Amerindian tribe, obviously took place over a period of time, Harris stresses the precipitate nature of the event; for Harris, the "trauma" of colonization is not so much an historical occurrence as a collapsing of history, a process in which the tribe's own "world-historical" view is displaced. The logic of this "phenomenal erosion" of time is indicated by the sequence "trauma of helplessness—external conquest, internal collapse." Colonization is experienced as a breach of the tribe's worldview, as a dislocation of their ability to witness what is happening to them.

This understanding of colonization as a precipitate collapse of time and space recalls his analysis of limbo and *vodun*, practices that bear "witness to a native suffering community *steeped* in caveats of conquest" (27; emphasis added), and an earlier essay in which he argues that "the environment of the Caribbean is steeped . . . in such broken conceptions as well as misconceptions of the meaning of conquest. No wonder [that] in the jungles of Guyana and Brazil, for example, material structural witnesses seem to exist in a terrible void of unreality" ("Tradition" 31). Harris's argument against realist representations of colonization parallels Lyotard's argument against the historicist representations of the Holocaust: such representations "chronologize" the fundamentally achronological time of trauma, thus disavowing the fact that a breach in time has ever taken place in the first place (Lyotard 17). The disjunctive temporality of Harris's novels is, by contrast, a mode of bearing witness to this breach. However, while Lyotard champions an art that emphasizes its own inability to witness trauma, Harris sees his art as a mode of belated witnessing. His position is closer to that of Dori Laub, who understands the Holocaust as "an event without witnesses" but suggests that the presence of an empathic listener enables a retroactive process of witnessing to take place (85). Harris concludes his essay by suggesting that the artist also occupies this position of the belated witness: "And this—as I see it—is also the role of the author within his ancestral background: he is the complex ghost of his own landscape of history or work . . . his poem or novel is subsistence of memory" ("Interior" 18).

Interceding in Time

Of the four novellas in *The Guyana Quartet*, *Palace of the Peacock* is the most complex witnessing of history, the closest that Harris comes to performing an act of critical history. The narrator or Dreamer travels from the coast to the interior, and from the present into the past, in order to visit his brother, Donne, whom he accompanies on a journey upriver in search of the "folk," the erstwhile inhabitants of the Mariella mission over whom Donne ruled and who have now disappeared into the bush. The journey upriver is a repetition of both "Donne's first innocent voyage and excursion" (27) in which he had first seduced his Amerindian mistress, also named Mariella, and of another voyage by a crew bearing exactly the same names as Donne's crew, who had been drowned to a man. The voyage also repeats the mythical search for El Dorado and Marlow's voyage up the Congo in *Heart of Darkness*. The narration of this colonial voyage is thus an explicit act of critical history, an attempt, as we shall see, both to relive and reverse the given conditions of the past. It is the Dreamer's presence as witness that allows this reversal to take place.

Instead of telling the story of a voyage that happened at a particular time and place in the past, the narrative stages a voyage that has repeated itself throughout history. Donne's pursuit of the folk is, for Harris, an "endless pursuit" (83), one that lures him and the crew to self-destruction. Although the crew members exhibit differing degrees of self-consciousness, and although they are partially aware that they are their own ghosts, they remain unable to break the cycle of repetition. Cameron, for instance, tells his fellow crew members that they are all "big frauds" "rise[n] bodily from the grave" (38) but remains enthralled by the repetitive logic of his own desire: "So it was, unwitting and ignorant, [Cameron] had been drawn to his death with the others, and had acquired the extraordinary defensive blindness, ribald as hell and witchcraft, of dying again and again to the world and still bobbing up once more lusting for an ultimate satisfaction and a cynical truth" (40). The trajectory of the narrative—as opposed to the trajectory of the voyage—is the translation of this "appetite for adventure" into "subsistence of memory," an alteration of perspective in which the crew are removed from their own desires and released from the process of "dying and dying again." In Nietzschean terms, one might say that they become aware of the law of eternal return. In Freudian terms, one might say that they become aware of their repetition compulsion.

However, this awareness is not simply a rational understanding of the cycle of repetition in which they are trapped, for such an understanding would merely satisfy the desire for "cynical truth" by leading to a nihilistic acceptance of their inability to alter their fate. Rather, it is a revelation of existence in which the world-weariness of being is transformed into the innocence of becoming, a revelation that goes beyond the nihilism of determinism insofar as it opens up for the crew "the ghost of a chance" of discarding their inherited nature. As we shall see, it is not simply a question of discarding one nature for another, of becoming a more moral subject. For this would merely be to repeat the bourgeois novel of education, centered around the progress of the individual subject, that Harris claims to move beyond. To abandon the "lust to rule" is in fact to abandon subjectivity itself. The goal of the Harrisian narrative is the dissolution rather than the education of the individual subject; the revelation of our "complex mutuality" destroys the (illusion of the) self even while it founds community.

The narrative is a redefinition of the nature of possibility. Early on in the novella, Donne advises the Dreamer to "Rule the land . . . while you still have the ghost of a chance" (23). In a later conversation, Donne begins to glimpse the alternative possibility that has been opened up by the presence of the Dreamer:

> "I have treated the folk badly," [Donne] admitted. "But you do know what this nightmare burden of responsibility adds up to, don't you? . . . I do wish," he spoke musingly, "someone would lift it from my shoulders. Maybe, who knows"—he was joking—"you can. . . . If [the folk] do murder me I've earned it I suppose, and I don't see sometimes how I can escape it *unless a different person steps into my shoes and accepts my confounded shadow.* . . . Still I suppose," he had grown thoughtful, "there's a ghost of a chance . . ."
>
> "Ghost of a chance of what?" I demanded, swept away by his curious rhetoric.
>
> "Changing my ways. . . . Perhaps there's a ghost of a chance that I can find a different relationship with the folk, who knows?" (51; emphasis added)

Donne's own history makes it impossible for him to be anything other than a tyrant, and yet this trip upriver, as a repetition of his previous voyage, offers him the ghost of a chance of rewriting history and of implanting in himself a "second nature" in opposition to his lust to rule. And, as Donne himself suggests, it is his brother, whom Donne describes as "this twin dreaming responsibility you remember" (23), who will make this act of critical history possible.

The dream sequence that begins the narrative already hints at the way in which the brother will function as Donne's creative conscience. In the first, Donne is shot by a hidden assassin. In the second, Mariella comes to the narrator's bedroom and lifts her dress to reveal where Donne has beaten her. And in the third the narrator connects the two previous dreams, concluding that Mariella is the hidden assassin of the first dream, that the slave-mistress has exacted her revenge on the master. The dreams thus function as an allegory of the imaginative act of empathy or witnessing that the narrative will itself become. In the first dream, the shot "pulled [the Dreamer] up and stifled [his] own heart in heaven" (19) as if he were taking the consequences of Donne's tyranny on himself. In the second, the Dreamer comes to inhabit both Donne's sexual desire for Mariella and Mariella's suffering. He reaches out to touch her wounds. She lifts her dress higher and "her convulsive sobbing stop[s] when [he] touche[s] her again" (21). Like Doubting Thomas, he verifies her suffering by touching her wounds, investing Donne's desire for Mariella with compassion but also implicating himself in Donne's "appetite": he is forced to see things through Donne's "dead seeing material eye rather than through [his own] living closed spiritual eye" (20).

In a more "straightforward" narrative the dream sequence would act as a mode of prophecy or warning. However, we later find out that Donne has already been shot by Mariella, just as the crew has already drowned. The Dreamer is thus the belated witness to events that have already happened. However, Harris's belief in the redemptive power of witnessing means that the narrator is able to *intercede in time*, intercede in the dialectic of master and slave and preempt the cycle of revenge. In the opening chapter of *Specters of Marx*, Derrida meditates on the relation between justice and vengeance via a reading of *Hamlet*. Hamlet's problem is that the ghost of his father equates justice with vengeance. This is the substance of Hamlet's famous complaint: "The time is out of joint. O cursed spite/That ever I was born to set it right!" (II i 189–90). Derrida argues that Hamlet's irresolution opens up the possibility of a justice that would not consist in taking revenge nor even in setting the time right—an essentially conservative action that would leave the social hierarchy intact—but in exploiting the time's out-of-jointness in order to conceive of a radically new mode of being: "If right or law stems from vengeance, as Hamlet seems to complain that it does . . . can one not yearn for a justice that one day, a day no longer belonging to history, a quasi-messianic day, would finally be removed from the fatality of vengeance?" (21). While the work of a secular novelist such as Coetzee can only rearticulate this longing, *Palace of the Peacock* constitutes an enactment of the quasi-messianic day itself. The shelving dream sequence that opens the narrative performs an active disjoining of time that opens up the possibility of Donne developing a new relation to Mariella and the folk. One might say that the repetition of Donne's "first innocent voyage and excursion" (27) takes place in a time of infinite hesitation, a time that does not so much defer as *dissolve* the retributive logic of the dream sequence.

The narrator's presence as witness reveals the "immaterial" presence of the folk: his redemptive vision turns the folk into the sacrificial Host. Like the Governor and the Amerindian king, the crew gradually become aware of their implication in the disappearance of the tribe/folk. Their desire or "appetite for adventure" is gradually transformed into a "new hunger" that moves beyond lust and progressively recognizes the sanctity of Mariella's body. Mariella's body becomes involved in a metonymic chain of substitutions in which her own profane body is transfigured first into the ambiguous "young-old" body of an Arawak woman who is pressed into service as the crew's guide and finally into the sacred body of the Virgin, whom Donne encounters in the Palace of the Peacock above the waterfall at the end of the river. In *Resurrection at Sorrow Hill*, Harris writes that "virgins in religions and myths are a measure of beleaguered conscience" (182). It is as if Harris's replaying of history allows the crew not only to atone for but also to undo the history of colonization. Harris transforms the traditional metaphor of the colonizing voyage upriver as a rape of the continent into a form of immaculate conception, as if his narrative were able to intervene in time and forestall what has already taken place.

This alternative outcome of the colonial voyage is not, however, simply escapism or wish fulfillment, but the insistence on a latent dimension or possibility within received history. Like Nietzsche's theory of eternal return, Harris's work reimagines history while simultaneously recognizing its infinite recurrence. If the Dreamer enables the crew to reimagine their voyage, he must also undergo their voyage exactly as it occurred. As in the initial dream sequence, this means that the Dreamer must "inhabit" their desire. Immediately prior to the capture of the Arawak woman, the Dreamer has another erotic dream from which he awakes in horror shouting: "the devil himself must fondle and mount this muse of hell and this hag" (43). The dream both "restore[s] to [him] Mariella's terrible stripes and anguish of soul" (43) and anticipates the crew's rape of the old Arawak woman. Hovering between remembrance and prophecy, it simultaneously signals the Dreamer's implication in and disaffiliation from the voyage of conquest. His physical presence on board the boat is no longer noted from this point on; like Tiresias in *The Waste Land*, his presence as empathic witness becomes commensurate with the act of narration itself.

The dream also presages the crew's own "disaffection": as the crew "enter" a narrow passage referred to as both "the straits of memory" (62) and "the War Office rapids" (63), the "ruffles in the water" become the Arawak woman's dress "rising and rolling to embrace the crew" (62), recalling the dress that Mariella lifts higher and higher in the initial dream sequence. As the old woman "displaces" Mariella in the crew's "affections," the violent nature of their desire is revealed. In the struggle to keep the bow straight, the crew become filled with a "murderous rape and fury" (63) and Carroll is lost over the side, almost as if his Amerindian blood means that he is the first to come to consciousness/conscience of the violent nature of their "adventure."

Carroll's relative innocence as "the youngest of the crew" (63) forces the rest of the men to reflect on the nature of their own responsibility/culpability, before they too, one by one, abandon ship. There is a slightly heavy-handed, unNietzschean moralism involved in this process of remembrance: for most of the crew, it involves a recognition of their responsibility as fathers and a vow to "do the right thing" by their mistresses. However the conventionality of this recognition is partially undercut by the fact that they are all already dead. Instead of a series of domestic reunions with individual members of "the folk," their homecoming is achieved only through their second deaths and their absorption into the selflessness of the "nameless and unflinching folk" (110).

The process by which Donne and the crew overcome their own natures is realized through a series of spatial images of ascension. As the crew travel deeper into the jungle, the steep cliff faces seem to offer the crew no way out of their destiny (the river is flowing far too fast for them to return downriver). But within the "parameters" of their journey, Harris discovers what he terms "fossils of creative possibility," a mythical residue that transforms each of their deaths into a form of rebirth. This is illustrated in the death of Wishrop, whose paddle catches a submerged rock and propels him up and out of the boat "like a man riding a wheel" (81). His hands later reemerge from the river like "fingers clinging to the spokes and spiders of a wheel" before he is lost to sight. The image of the wheel implicitly suggests the possibility of Wishrop's eventual ascension, a suggestion that is echoed by the reference to spider worship or anancy. In "History, Fable and Myth," Harris reminds us of the folkloric association between anancy, limbo dancing, and the cramped conditions in the holds of the Middle Passage. Harris's spider imagery thus becomes a mode of prophecy, a promise of Wishrop's eventual rebirth.

The trajectory of Wishrop's ejection from the boat then suggests an alternative mode of ascension to Vigilance, another member of the crew, who looks up at the cliffs and sees "a spidery skeleton crawling to the sky" (82). Soon afterward, with "all blind lust and obfuscation . . . banished from his mind" (85), he is literally able to rise above the voyage by climbing up the canyon side together with the Arawak woman. His dreaming ascension, in which he acquires both "immateriality and mysterious substantiality" (82), affords him a revelatory perspective. He is able to see the boat below him as both "the childish repetitive boat and prison of life" (83) and as the "naked spider of spirit" (81). In other words, he is able to see both the fruitless, repetitive nature of their voyage and its redemptive potential. His perspective thus comes to parallel that of the Dreamer, who also looks down on the boat from Vigilance's "god-like perch" (92).

But this movement of ascension needs to be distinguished from a drive toward abstraction. Rather, Harris's "view from above" needs to be placed within a dialectical tradition of remembrance that attempts to traverse the distance between the history and the historian. Like Benjamin's Angel, positioned halfway between heaven and earth, spirit and matter, Harris's narrators bear witness to history as catastrophe while simultaneously insisting that "every second of time was the straight gate through which the Messiah might enter" ("Theses" 264).

Although at first sight the final section of the novella seems to resemble the celebration of a heavenly "back world," it is in fact a redemption *of* rather than *from* history, a remembrance rather than a forgetting of material suffering. The section is entitled "Paling of Ancestors." While the epigraph from Gerald Manley Hopkins, "This piece-bright paling shuts the spouse/Christ home, Christ and his mother and all his hallows" (97), emphasizes the Christian dimensions of this title, the word *paling* was initially used to describe the boundary fence that separated the part of Ireland under British rule from the rest of Ireland.[10] Christ's home turns out to be in barbarian territory. Because Harris's vision of liberation operates on a political level as well as a spiritual one, it becomes possible to read the final section as a mode of communion that brings into being a collective, a mode of mourning that announces—in that liminal space between self and other, chartered and unchartered territory—the possibility of community.

Of the crew, only Donne and one of the Da Silva twins make it to the waterfall at the head of the river. During his ascent of the waterfall (by another ladder), Donne is finally afforded a revelation of "the unselfness of night, the invisible otherness around . . . [and] his own nothingness" (108), before he and Da Silva slip and fall to their deaths. Only after he has come to an under-standing of his own immateriality is Donne able to "come home at last to the unflinching compassion of the folk" (110). The spirits of the dead crew are summoned by the sound of Carroll's whistle, a whistle that differs from the trumpet that awakens the dead on the Day of Judgment in that its music sum-mons without judgment or discrimination. Unlike the Christian prophecy, Harris's vision is not structured by the dualism of this world and the next, heaven and hell. The narrator likens Carroll's whistle to the cry of the peacock. As Michael Gilkes notes, the peacock's multicolored wings are an alchemical symbol of unity-in-diversity. Although this sounds like a version of multicul-tural community, it is important to remember that the community being imag-ined here is not a community of subjects. It is perhaps closer to the anti-foun-dationalist type of community imagined by Jean-Luc Nancy in *The Inoperative Community:* "If community is revealed in the death of others it is because death itself is the true community of 'I's that are not egos. It is not a communion that fuses the egos into an Ego or a higher We. It is the community of others" (15).

And what brings into being this communion of others turns out to be the trace of a mourning ritual: latent within the music of Carroll's whistle is, as Harris himself later noted in "Introduction to *The Guyana Quartet*" (9), the music of the Carib bone flute. This is not only a community of others, then, but a *communion* of others in which the drive to consume that underwrites the history of modernity is transformed into a collective ethic of subsistence. The absorption of the crew into "one muse and undying soul" is not a "drive toward abstraction" or transcendence but rather a moment of transubstantiation, a memorialization of the other as "universal morsel": "I felt the faces before me begin to fade and part company from themselves as if our need of one another was now fulfilled, and our distance from one another was the distance of sacrament" (117).

AFTER-TEXTS

I want to conclude this chapter by comparing the final movement of *Palace of the Peacock* with the final movement of Coetzee's *Foe*, both of which take the reader into an extradiscursive, extrahistorical space. Coetzee's narrative offers a materialist, antiredemptive glimpse of Friday's "home" in the sunken wreck of a slave ship. By the end of *Foe*, Friday's body remains essentially the same inscrutable object. The way in which the narrative falls away, unable to assign a meaning to this abject body, led me to describe the last movement of the novel as a kind of after-text. But this after-text is precisely not an afterlife: when the nonnarrator descends beneath the surface of the waves, he encounters Friday's corpse rather than his soul. While I have suggested that Coetzee's narrators move toward some sort of obscure *rapprochement* with the other, this *rapprochement* is not the traditional empathic identification with the other as same but an abject identification with the difference of the other, an antitranscendent encounter with the other as object, as that which has been relegated to the realm of the subhuman.

Palace of the Peacock moves in the opposite direction. Immediately following the initial dream sequence, we lose sight of Mariella's abused body. The fluidity of identity that characterizes Harris's dream narratives does not leave room to acknowledge the specificity of her suffering: her body is merely the first in a chain of substitutions. The transition from Mariella to the nameless Arawak woman to Mary would constitute a progressive loss of difference, a movement in which she is Anglicized and Christianized, were it not for the fact that she is not fully individuated in the first place. Harris's intention is to provide a merger rather than an encounter between subject and object, text and world, a dissolution of borders that allows both Mariella and the crew to become "one with the undivided soul and anima of the universe" (116). This merger of transubstantiated souls is very different from Coetzee's nonnarrator's frustrated wrestling with Friday's forgotten corpse. While *Foe* attempts to remember that which has been excluded from memory, *Palace of the Peacock* ends in a vision of universal memorialization in which nothing is forgotten, a mode of spiritual being which—unlike the Christian conception of heaven—is not predicated on a zone of unbeing.

While both endings function as modes of remembering the dead, Coetzee's remains uncompromising in its refusal to console. To reach the "home of

Friday" is to recognize that the desire of the narrative—to recover Friday's story—must remain perpetually unfulfilled: the nonnarrator's question "what is this ship?" goes unanswered. By contrast, Harris's narrative journey arrives at its spiritual destination, its home in the folk, because it is able to transmute the desire of its passengers into love. For Harris, to remain inconsolable would be to succumb to despair and nihilism, to refuse to recognize the potential of art to provide a kind of restitution or consolation. For the Dreamer, the ending is "the dance of all fulfillment [which] I now held and knew deeply, cancelling my forgotten fear of strangeness and catastrophe in a destitute world" (116). For Coetzee's nonnarrator, it is precisely his awareness of the "destitute world" that threatens to cancel his art.

Nevertheless, despite these differences, the work of both writers serves to heighten our sense of the impossible necessity of doing justice to the memory of the dead. This contradictory obligation is at the heart of Geoffrey Hartman's sense of the impossibility of compiling a Book of Destruction in memory of the Shoah: "Our *sefer hashoah* [Book of Destruction] will have to accomplish the impossible: allow the limits of representation to be healing limits yet not allow them to conceal an event we are obligated to recall and interpret" (334). In their very different explorations of the limits of representation, both Coetzee and Harris are responding to the same unresolvable tension between mourning and melancholia, between the need to come to terms with the past and the need never to forget.

CHAPTER THREE

Keeping It in the Family

Passing on Racial Memory in the Novels of Toni Morrison

Jazz always keeps you on edge. There is no final chord. There may be a long chord, but no final chord. And it agitates you. . . . [Jazz musicians] have the ability to make you want [more], and to remember the want. That is a part of what I want to put in my books. They will never fully satisfy—never fully.
                                        —Toni Morrison, qtd. in McKay

In addition to having to use their heads to get ahead, they had the weight of the whole race sitting there. You needed two heads for that.
                                        —Toni Morrison, *Beloved*

But who misleads my voice? Who grates
my voice? Stuffing my throat
with a thousand bamboo fangs?
      —Aimé Césaire, "Notebook of a Return to the Native Land"[1]

Toni Morrison suggests that her determination to make her readers "remember the want" is part of what defines her writing as black. Although some degree of working through takes place within her novels, enabling individuals to come to terms with their personal histories, a racial memory of an "ungovernable" loss (122) prevents her novels from offering closure. Throughout her work, and especially in *Beloved*, the weighty memory of an injustice

79

done to the whole race constitutes a physical impediment to mourning, a memory of a violence done to the black body that, as in Césaire's tortured manifesto of black consciousness, functions as a speech impediment, blocking the process of verbalization and mourning.

If Morrison's novels function on one level as the narrativization of African American experience, as a form of *cultural* memory, on another level they encounter the materiality of *racial* memory.[2] In order to understand the role of remembrance in *Beloved*, it is necessary to draw this distinction between a cultural memory that comprises the verbal—both written and oral, official and unofficial—accounts of a community's history, and a racial memory that remains nonverbalized yet somehow passes itself on from generation to generation, as if it were secretly encrypted within the cultural text. Because the "weight of the whole race" cannot be accommodated within consciousness, it passes itself on from generation to generation as symptom or affect. It passes itself on as a *memory of the body*, a memory of the violence inflicted on the racially marked body, that is also a *bodily memory*, a memory that takes on a bodily form precisely because it exceeds both the individual's and the community's capacity for verbalization and mourning.

This distinction between cultural and racial memory disturbs the utopian symmetry of multiculturalist discourses in which every citizen can lay claim to a distinct "ethnic" identity grounded in a particular cultural history. The term "ethnicity" is often preferred over the term "race" because it emphasizes cultural over biological inheritance.[3] But this preference often amounts to a disavowal of the reality of racism and leads to the impression that we are all equally "ethnic." It denies the fact that "consciousness of the body is solely a negating activity" (Fanon 110) for the nonwhite subject. As Kalpana Seshadri-Crooks has argued, whites do not undergo the same negation as nonwhites because whiteness functions as a naturalized sign of the human, as a nonsignifier of race. While all subjects are in possession of a cultural memory, only the racially marked are truly in possession of a racial memory, of what amounts to an inherited memory of collective negation.[4]

While cultural memory can be assimilated into the individual consciousness as a complement to the individual's sense of identity, racial memory threatens to destroy this sense of identity by dissolving the individual within a collective experience of negation. Cultural memory is a "healthy" mode of remembrance, a mode of commemoration that is essentially self-centered in that it is a way of claiming the dead, of claiming one's ancestry, in order to shore up one's identity in the present. Racial memory, by contrast, is "unhealthy" insofar as it is a melancholic identification *with* the dead, a life-threatening, other-centered mode of being claimed *by* the dead, a mode of being-for-death. Like the melancholia of Friday and Michael K, racial memory is a way of identifying with the way in which one's ancestors have been forgotten—even while they were alive. For African Americans, it is a way of identifying with the nameless victims of the Middle Passage and slavery, with the way in which the institution of slavery was founded on the foreclosure of the slave's humanity.

In *Moses and Monotheism,* Freud describes this collective memory of a Forgetting as a phylogenetic inheritance. Paralleling his attempts elsewhere to describe the psychic life of the individual, Freud employs the seemingly biological term "phylogenetic" for precisely the same reason that I have recourse to the term "racial memory": not in order to reinvoke the specter of biological determinism that has haunted the development of both psychoanalysis and race theory, but in order to indicate that the psychic life of the collective is not wholly to be accounted for as a cultural phenomenon, in order to indicate the *materiality* of the collective unconscious. Freud's essay treads a fine line between biological and cultural determinism and between a universalist and a relativist construction of the human psyche. His positing of a "primal scene" in which the Israelites murdered Moses can be taken as evidence of his desire either to posit a universal prehistory for mankind—elsewhere he suggests that all societies are founded on a similar murder of the father—or to account for the difference of Jewish culture. What is radical in Freud's thinking here is that he shows how an unhistoricizable (historically unverifiable) event secretly determines the specificity of Judaeo-Christian history.

Freud's controversial last work is itself secretly determined by the historical conditions under which Freud wrote. Freud attempts to tell his story of the Jews at precisely the time of their greatest persecution; the third part of the book is written after he himself is forced to flee to England.[5] The question of the historical identity of the Jewish tribe is thus irrevocably bound up with the question of anti-Semitism, the origin of the race with the origin of racism. It is precisely because the history of the Jewish "race" is inextricably tied to a history of racism that African Americans have identified their own history of oppression and exile with that of the Jews. However, here I am less interested in the similar content of the two "tribal" histories than in the way in which this history is transmitted. Freud distinguishes between the textual biblical narrative that we usually think of as constituting the memory of the Jewish tribe and a memory that the biblical narrative attempts to conceal, a memory that is passed on to future generations as a secret, as if it were lodged in the "body" of the biblical text. This memory manifests itself as symptom, as a compulsion to repeat the "original" act of patricide. It is as if a history of oppression can only inscribe itself in the unconscious as a guilty memory, as if the only way to claim the history of what was done to the race is to claim responsibility for the violation, to store it as the memory of a self-inflicted violence. To register—or more accurately, to fail to register—a violence done to the race as a collective act of patricide is a way of keeping it, so to speak, in the family.

The claustrophobic, often incestuous nature of violence in Morrison's novels testifies to this perverse desire to keep the memory of racial abuse in the family—or at least within the community. The traumatic, unspeakable secrets around which each novel is structured are acts of familial, black-on-black violence. I am thinking of Cholly's rape of his own daughter in *The Bluest Eye;* of Eva's cremation of her still-living son and the National Suicide Day procession that ends up burying itself alive in *Sula;* of the life insurance salesman's suicide flight and Milkman's leap into the "killing arms of his brother" (331) in *Song of Solomon;* of the violently abusive relationship between Son and Jadine in *Tar Baby;* of Sethe's infanticide in *Beloved;* of Joe's murder of his lover and his wife's knifing of her corpse in *Jazz;* and of a black town's lynching of a community of women whom they see as a threat to their moral and racial purity in *Paradise.* Morrison's latest novel makes particularly clear the logic that governs all these acts of (self)-destruction: the black community inflicts on itself—*acts out*—that part of its history which it has been unable to digest. Each act of self-inflicted or familial violence is a way of remembering—while not remembering—the violence done to the whole race.

While each novel performs an important work of cultural memory by narrativizing a specific era of African American history, each novel also refers back to an "original" violation that is not fully locatable within the historical time frame of the narrative, a violation that comes to function as a prehistory to the events of the narrative. In Morrison's early fiction, the violation is located within the prehistory of individual characters, in Cholly's childhood "rape" at the hands of two white men and in the extreme poverty that leads Eva to sacrifice her own leg in order to feed her children. In later novels, this prior violation acquires an increasingly mythic or primal status as it is pushed further and further back into the prehistory of the narrative. In *Song of Solomon,* the characters' actions can be traced back to the lynching of the first Macon Dead; in *Tar Baby* to the slave economy upon which Valerian's candy empire is built; in *Beloved* to the Middle Passage and the rape of Sethe's own mother; in *Jazz* to the history of lynchings and miscegenation that Joe and Violet attempt to escape by moving North; and in *Paradise* to the time of the "Disallowing" (194), the series of rejections that a black town's founding fathers experience in their search for a home during the era of Reconstruction. It is no coincidence that Morrison has recourse first to actual African American myths (of the flying African in *Song of Solomon* and Brer Rabbit's encounter with a Tar Baby in *Tar Baby*), and then to events in African American history whose apocalyptic proportions lend them the status of mythic narratives. The psychologically unregisterable nature of these latter events removes them from the world of historically verifiable fact and renders them, to borrow Denver's description/explanation of her sister, "more" (*Beloved* 266). The excessive nature of this racial memory brings to crisis the historicizing impulse of each narrative by acknowledging the presence of a "primal" history that the narrative is unable to access directly, a history that threatens to overwhelm the narrative's ability to mourn and commemorate.

What, then, is the status of Morrison's narratives? Do they constitute a mode of acting out the traumatic memory of racial violence, or are they a mode of working through this memory? Are they works of mourning or melancholia? Clearly, in laying bare the logic of repetition, in revealing, for instance, how Cholly's rape of his daughter is the consequence of his own "rape" at the hands of two white men, Morrison's novels constitute a mode of working through. Nevertheless, because the injustices of slavery and its aftermath can never be fully worked through, because racial oppression remains a contemporary reality, because the cycle of (self-)abuse and violation is still playing itself out in black communities across the United States, the narratives are unable to offer closure. As cultural memory, her novels are a crucial mode of commemorating African American history; as racial memory, they serve to indicate how this history threatens to collapse into itself, how it threatens to become what Cathy Caruth, in her reading of *Moses and Monotheism*, describes as "the history of a trauma" (185).

Morrison's work refuses to close the wound of African American history in recognition of the impossibility of ever fully coming to terms with the history of racism, the impossibility of abreacting an "event" that did not take place at a singular, historically specific moment in time. In Freud's classic account of individual trauma, Emma enters a store, hears someone laughing and suffers a massive attack of anxiety. It later transpires in analysis that she was molested in the store as a child and repressed all conscious knowledge of the event. Although it is not clear that Emma or other trauma victims can ever be entirely "cured," some sort of progress is usually made if the anxiety attack can be explained (away) by locating and referencing the "original" traumatic event. However, if Emma were black and the storeowner white, she may well suffer a massive attack of anxiety even if she was never personally molested in the store, even if she was literally not present at the scene of the original molestation. The origin of her trauma is not to be located within the confines of the individual case history, but rather within a collective history of racial abuse, a history that is not so much a history as a suspension of history, an infinite repetition of the original scene of molestation. Such a "history" can never be abreacted or adequately mourned.

Just as racial memory constantly threatens to invade personal memory, personal memories of racism, unassimilated by the individual consciousness, become part of an impersonal collective memory—a memory of impersonalization. Because racism denies the specificity of the racially marked subject, the experience of racial abuse remains, in Caruth's phrase, "unclaimable" by the individual.[6] This is exactly what Sethe attempts to explain to Denver when she tells her that "Sweet Home is going to always be there waiting for you" (36). Because Sethe was unable to process her experiences of racial abuse, the experience remains "out there," a material presence that other (racially marked) people might "bump into" (36). While most critics have accounted for Sethe's inability to believe in (the passing of) time in terms of personal trauma, Sethe makes it clear that her memory of Sweet Home is transpersonal and nonhistorical:

> I used to think it was my rememory. You know. Some things you forget and other things you never do. But it's not. . . . Where I was before I came here, that place is real. It's never going away. Even if the whole farm— every tree and grass blade of it—dies. The picture is still there and what's more, if you go there—you who never was there—if you go and stand in the place where it was, it will happen again. (35–36)

Although she then seeks to protect Denver by telling her "you can't never go there," her real fear is that "there" will once again come to 124. She cannot admit to her daughter that 124 is also Real in the Lacanian sense, also the site of an event that she is unable to assimilate into the temporal framework of her life, an event that thus constantly threatens to repeat itself. The progress of the narrative thus cannot be that of the conventional case history, in which Sethe would belatedly experience that which she was not able to experience at the time of its occurrence and thus cure herself of her inability to believe in time. Sethe's experiences cannot be reclaimed because they lie outside the framework of the human, past the limit of what one is able to endure and still remain human. Narrative progression consists rather in getting the inhabitants of 124 to understand that "there [is] no defense" (244), in reconciling them to the ever-present threat of invasion. What I hope to demonstrate in offering yet another reading of *Beloved* is that, for the racially marked, *coming to terms with one's personal history involves reconciling oneself to the fact that one can never come to terms with one's collective history.*

THE CRITICAL CONSENSUS: RECLAIMING A HISTORY

The critical reception of Morrison's work is too voluminous to summarize with any degree of accuracy. Those who have attempted this task have tended to organize their accounts according to the critics' various theoretical persuasions (Peach) or by subject matter (Matus) without attempting to arbitrate between the readings produced by the diverse critical persuasions of the critics. The problem is exacerbated by the reluctance of individual critics to engage with one another; each seems content to claim Morrison for his or her own without explicitly contesting other critics' readings of Morrison's work.

Nevertheless, it does seem possible to speak of a broad critical consensus. Influenced at least in part by the Black Aesthetic Movement of the 1960s, most critics have presented Morrison's novels as a reclamation of black history and identity. Despite the attempts of critics such as Henry Louis Gates to complicate the "critical paradigms" of this movement, the "assumption that black literature has a role in countering negative assumptions of black people and in promoting black consciousness informs much of the critical writing" on Morrison (Peach 5). Although a number of critics have employed postmodern, poststructuralist and psychoanalytic approaches, "there is . . . a pervasive unease . . . about the appropriateness of contemporary European critical methodologies to African American writing" (Peach 5). Critics have thus been at pains to present their readings within the context of an African American political aesthetic, and few have sought to directly challenge the assumptions of that aesthetic.

Although many critics have emphasized the traumatic elements of Morrison's work, they have still tended to read her novels as redemptive works of mourning, commemoration and recovery rather than as works of melancholia. Mae Henderson's 1991 essay "Toni Morrison's *Beloved:* Re-Membering the Body as Historical Text" is exemplary in this regard. Presenting Morrison alternately as a historian, a psychoanalyst and an archaeologist, Henderson argues that Morrison's "work is intended to *resurrect* stories *buried* and *express* stories *repressed*" (63). Like many other critics indebted to New Historicism, Henderson has recourse to a number of poststructuralist thinkers while ignoring their critique of historicism.[7] For instance, she includes a passage from Derrida's *Mémoires for Paul de Man* that appears to indicate that Derrida is affirming the need for mourning. In her bid to enlist support for what she sees as "Morrison's . . . project of recovery and 'rememory'" (83), she completely fails to note that the passage from *Mémoires* is actually part of an anti-historicist *critique* of mourning.

One of the few critics to question the canonical reading of *Beloved* (or indeed of Morrison's entire oeuvre) as an act of historical reclamation is Roger Luckhurst. Although he does not explicitly contest Henderson's essay, he returns to *Mémoires* in order to argue that Morrison, like Derrida, recognizes the limits of mourning and historicism, most notably in her recognition of the impossibility of ever fully coming to terms with the genocide of the Middle Passage. Luckhurst's description of the ghost-child Beloved as "a brute materiality that resists symbolisation, and thus forever disrupts mourning" (245) anticipates my own sense of Beloved as that which exceeds memorialization. In highlighting the importance of the Lacanian Real to a consideration of mourning in *Beloved,* Luckhurst underscores precisely that which the New Historicist reading seeks to gloss over. As Joan Copjec has argued, despite their adoption of a poststructuralist vocabulary, New Historicists typically refuse the notion that "something will forever remain inarticulable in any historical text" (ix). The present chapter seeks to emphasize the importance of the Real, not so much as an aporia that structures "any historical text" but as that which is *produced* by the specificities of African American history. My intention is not so much to historicize the Real (a logical impossibility) as to investigate the ways in which certain historical events elude symbolic registration and thus assume the primal proportions—the haunting power—of myth.

More recently, Jill Matus has also contested the critical orthodoxy, in her 1998 study of trauma in Morrison's novels. Like Luckhurst, she does not explicitly present her argument as a challenge to critical orthodoxy, perhaps because her book is meant to function, as the series editor puts it, as "an authoritative introduction" (xi) rather than a polemical critical monograph. Her argument is most discernible when she probes Morrison's own view of her work. In her 1993 Nobel acceptance speech, Morrison mounts a critique of memorialization, which she associates with "the sentimentality and nostalgia needed for nation-building and forgetting" (Matus 15). Matus then quietly adds "one question that can be put to her novels is whether the language involved in producing cultural memory can ever be exempt from the dangerous task of memorializing" (15). Without drawing explicit attention to the inconsistencies within Morrison's view of her own project, Matus later notes how Morrison, in "A Bench by the Road," conceives of *Beloved* as a memorial to those who died during the Middle Passage (30). In a postscript on *Paradise*, Matus implicitly suggests that this inconsistency can be accounted for as part of Morrison's evolution as a novelist: while "*Song of Solomon* dealt with the need for prideful history" (161), *Paradise* explores the dangers of excessive commemoration, as "a symptom of enduring trauma" (155). Matus's own argument attempts a partial reconciliation of this contradiction: "As much as Morrison's novels constitute a form of cultural memory . . . they also disclaim the possibility of entirely transforming painful, unassimilated history into satisfactorily integrated narrative" (36).

Finally my argument also builds on Barbara Freeman's contention that "the challenge at stake in *Beloved* is not to recover a repressed or forgotten past, but rather to represent an absence" (129). While I am in broad agreement with her argument that "Beloved enacts the sublime" (136) by functioning as a "bridge" that allows the other characters "access to a past that is strictly speaking irretrievable" (137), her contention that "mourning consists in sustaining rather than severing our continuing love for the dead" (139) ignores the life-threatening consequences of Sethe's inability to sever her ties to Beloved. Her desire to celebrate what she terms a "feminine sublime" leads her to valorize the connection between language and the body which my own analysis of what one might term a racial sublime leads me to present as part of the problem.[8]

My distinction between cultural and racial memory is an attempt to render explicit that which the canonical historicist reading has glossed over, namely the tension in Morrison's oeuvre between memorialization and antimemorialization, mourning and melancholia. In arguing that we need to supplement our understanding of cultural memory with a theory of racial memory, I hope to show how racial identity is partly grounded on what we are *unable* to remember and reclaim.

THE BODY AND REMEMBRANCE

In seeking to reveal the limits of mourning, I also hope to clarify the status of the body in Morrison's text: for the vast majority of critics, and in particular for feminist critics, Morrison's materialist poetics is aligned with the project of remembering the suffering of the black body. The conflation of body and text implicit in the title of Henderson's essay is echoed in that of one of the most widely disseminated articles on *Beloved*, Jean Wyatt's "Giving Body to the Word: The Maternal Symbolic in Toni Morrison's *Beloved*," published in *PMLA* (1993). My own emphasis on racial memory seeks to question this alignment of the word and the body by insisting that memories lodge themselves in the body precisely because they cannot be verbalized, that Morrison has recourse to a language of the body precisely in order to indicate that which defies mourning.

In order to present Morrison's body language as a mode of affirmation, Wyatt has to revise the conventional psychoanalytic understanding of the relationship between language and the body. Thus she argues that Morrison contests Lacan's association of the symbolic order of language with absence and the paternal function of severance and replaces it with a "maternal symbolic" in which language reinforces presence and connection. Wyatt's argument parallels Freeman's assertion that mourning rather than melancholia is a way of maintaining connection. Freeman revises Freud and Wyatt Lacan in tacit agreement with the project of *écriture féminine*, which celebrates the liberating potential of a bodily, precultural and nonpatriarchal language. Crucial to the project of *écriture féminine* is an affirmation of motherhood and of the preverbal bond between mother and child. However, *Beloved* reveals how this "oceanic" space can prove, for African Americans, essentially dystopian rather than utopian. Regression into a preverbal state is a regression not only into the safety of the womb but also into the terrifyingly vulnerable state of "captive flesh" (Spillers 68), a place where mother love is liable to express itself in acts not of nurturing but of infanticide.

According to Lacanian orthodoxy, behind the Imaginary mother of creativity, presence and connection celebrated by *écriture féminine* lurks the destructive figure of the Real mother, to whom I shall return later on in this chapter. I take issue with Wyatt and Freeman not out of a dogmatic belief in the universal validity of the Lacanian schema but precisely because the traumatic dimensions of slavery and the Middle Passage call for an emphasis on the Real rather than the Imaginary, precisely because the specificities of African American history sharpen rather than blur the distinction between absence and presence, language and the body, mourning and melancholia. As William Handley argues, *Beloved* demonstrates how the deconstructive/psychoanalytic understanding of "language-as-loss is not only a culturally relative concept but *produced by history*—specifically, for African American culture, the history of slavery" (679; emphasis added).

The relevance of Lacan's emphasis on the materiality of trauma to African American subject formation is convincingly demonstrated in Hortense Spillers' historiographical essay, "Mama's Baby, Papa's Maybe: An African-American Grammar Book."[9] In her analysis of how slavery mandates the slave's "absence from a subject position" (67), Spillers argues that slavery reduces the slave body to flesh, "that zero degree of socialization" (67). The slave body is no longer the sign of the human but regresses to a precultural, ungendered state of "total objectification" (68). Forcibly removed from one (African) cultural order, slaves are denied entry into another (that of the New World) except as objects of exchange. Slavery constitutes a "theft of the body" insofar as it deprives the slave of the right to "name" his/her own flesh and its issue—a theft that relegates the slave to a "vestibular" position outside the sociolinguistic order (67). Slavery and the Middle Passage thus function as the prehistory of the African American subject, a prehistory that endlessly threatens to reoccur. "Even though the captive flesh/body has been 'liberated,' and no one need pretend that the quotation marks do not matter . . . it is as if neither time nor history . . . shows movement, as the human subject is 'murdered' over and over again" by a language that "remains grounded in the originating metaphors of captivity and mutilation" (68).

My emphasis on racial memory is designed to steer my analysis away from a pseudoanalytic reduction of the novel to a series of case histories and toward an understanding of Morrison's work as constituting its own analysis of a racially inherited collective trauma. While I do offer accounts of the principal characters' emergence from the "unbeing" of slavery, I do so without positing in advance a particular model of subjectivity to which they ought to lay claim. By limiting Lacan's conception of the "speaking subject" to someone who remains open to the question of what it means to be human, or more specifically what it means to be either a man or a woman, I hope to avoid the Foucauldian objection to psychoanalysis as necessarily reliant on a particular version of the human. Similarly, the Lacanian category of the Real is a

metapsychological concept that marks the limits of psychoanalytic understanding, the point at which psychoanalysis drops its claim to be a science and
enters the realm of speculation and myth. Thus in placing his story (Freud's)
alongside hers (Morrison's) I seek to show the point where both stories
encounter their own limits as explanatory discourses.

Fanon himself struggled with the question of the universality of psychoanalysis, drawing on Freud and Lacan but noting, for instance, that "the
Oedipus complex is far from coming into being among Negroes" (152). In
opposition to Mannoni, who sought to prove a universal "dependency complex" suffered by all colonized peoples, Fanon sought to restore the Malagasy's
dream of threatening black men to *"its proper time"* and *"place,"* namely colonial Madagascar and the French use of Senegalese police to repress and exter-
minate the natives. Thus a certain historicizing impulse is crucial in resisting
the temptation to generalize across different cultures. Nevertheless, it seems
equally important to avoid the assumption that historical knowledge produces
a complete understanding of the dreams of the Malagasy. A definitive analysis would have to take into account the specificities of the lives lived out by
each individual Malagasay, who may or may not have first-hand experience of
Senegalese oppression, as well as the complex ways in which individual experiences of Senegalese violence become part of a collective racial memory. In
endeavoring to restore the dreams of Morrison's characters to their proper
time and place, we will necessarily come against the elusive temporality of
trauma and thus the limits of historicism.

Spillers's analysis of slavery clarifies the link between Beloved's identity
as the ghost of Sethe's preverbal infant and her collective identity as the trace
of the "Sixty Million and more" victims of slavery and the Middle Passage.
Sethe's infanticide inadvertently consigns Beloved to the same precultural
limbo as the slave; when she returns to the world of the living she carries with
her traumatic memories of a place of undifferentiated bodies that suggests the
material conditions onboard the slave ships. On the one hand, then, Beloved
carries with her memories of the historic (or rather prehistoric) violence done
to the black body during the Middle Passage, the place where, as she recounts
in her monologue, it is impossible to mourn: "if we had more to drink we
could make tears" (210). On the other, she is herself a bodily memory, a memory that has taken on flesh.

Morrison suggests that "the purpose of making the ghost real is making
history possible, making memory real" (qtd. in Darling 249). In other words,
incarnating the past in the form of Beloved enables the characters (and the
readers) to confront the past, "making it possible to remember" the past "in a
manner in which it can be digested" (248). However, Beloved's material presence also clearly indicates the failure of mourning, the *in*digestibility of the
memory of slavery; she returns precisely because, like those who died during

the Middle Passage, she has been, in Morrison's phrase, "unceremoniously buried" (244). She returns in the flesh because her death has not been adequately symbolized or put into words.

A FAILURE TO NAME

Sethe is allowed to attend the physical burial of Beloved but not the funeral ceremony itself. When she is released from prison, she belatedly erects a tombstone, but the word she has engraved on the tombstone fails to function as an epitaph, fails to perform the symbolic function of naming—and mourning—what is lost. The word is part of the only phrase that Sethe was able to take in at the burial, the opening words of the preacher's address: "Dearly Beloved" (184). As part of an address to a collective, the epigraph anticipates the collective identity that "Beloved" has acquired by the time she returns to the world of the living. The word also names Sethe's *undying affection*. The tombstone and its epitaph function to memorialize or monumentalize Sethe's undying mother love rather than the dead child. In Lacanian terms, this means that Beloved remains caught between two births: her natural birth and her birth into language, and two deaths: her natural death and its symbolization.[10] And Sethe herself is caught within the same limbo; with "her knees wide open as the grave" (5), she surrenders both her body and her subjectivity. Having opened up a passageway between the living and the dead, she can no longer claim for herself a separate identity; she loses herself in what Michèle Montrelay dubs the "infinite placenta time" of mother and preverbal infant, the "too-full" time-space of pregnancy and nursing in which the mother "cannot say that she is two even less that she is one," a time-space which, like the digits of Sethe's address ("124"), subverts "the habitual mode of counting" (Montrelay 85).

Thus when the baby returns, the women of 124 find themselves "locked in a love that wore everybody out" (243), a love that literally wears away Sethe's presence. As the incarnation of a name that is not a name, Beloved draws Sethe and Denver into a preverbal world where words become objects of consumption, ways of feeding—but never satiating—Beloved's demand for recognition. As Slavoj Žižek writes, "The apparitions that emerge in the domain between two deaths address to us some unconditional demand, and it is for this reason that they incarnate pure drive without desire" (*Sublime Object* 108). The monologues that Wyatt refers to as "Morrison's song of desire" (480) are in fact the attempt to articulate this pure drive without desire—for desire cannot exist in the absence of separation—a desire that inexorably reveals itself as a death drive: like Michael K's attempt to remember his forgotten mother, Sethe's attempt to remember her daughter leads to the disappearance of her own body.

In attempting to meet Beloved's insatiable demand, Sethe almost turns *herself* into a ghost. Beloved grows bigger and bigger as she absorbs Sethe's love and grows pregnant with the child that Paul D had promised Sethe. Beloved physically deprives Sethe of her maternal body; as Beloved grows more and more "material," Sethe dematerializes: "The flesh between [Sethe's] forefinger and thumb was thin as china silk and there wasn't a piece of clothing in the house that didn't hang on her" (239). This process of dematerialization is psychically necessary in that it deprives Sethe of what Wyatt accurately describes as her "monumental" maternal body (476). But it is not clear that Sethe is capable of surviving this demonumentalization of her body. Beloved's excessive presence, which fills 124 with the indigestible memories of the "Sixty Million and more," literally renders Sethe *incapable of digestion*. It is only when Sethe "spit[s] up something she had not eaten" (243), that Denver begins to understand that "her mother could die" and goes to seek help from the women of the community, from the world of the living. It is only the power of *their* collective voice—as opposed to that of the women of 124—that is able to dematerialize and "disremember" Beloved and reclaim the (barely) living from the dead. Beloved has to be exorcised—spat out—into the epilogue precisely because of the intolerable nature of her claim on the living.

Just as Sethe is forced to relinquish her attempt to meet Beloved's infinite claim, Morrison is similarly forced to relinquish her attempt to reclaim the "Sixty Million and more" to whom the novel is dedicated. The line breaks that Morrison introduces into the biblical prose of her epigraph already suggest the unbridgeable caesura of the Middle Passage: "I will call them my people/who were not my people/and her beloved/who was not beloved" (Romans: 9: 25). Insofar as the epigraph draws an analogy between God's ability to call His people unto him and her own ability to do likewise, it already hints at the hubristic proportions of the task she has set herself. And by the epilogue, Morrison is forced to recognize the impossibility of naming and reclaiming the nameless: "Disremembered and unaccounted for, she cannot be lost because no one is looking for her, and even if they were, how could they call her if they don't know her name. Although she has claim, she is not claimed" (274). Because she lacks a proper name by which she might be remembered, Beloved can never be properly buried and must remain "a loneliness that roams" (274).

In order to read the novel as a reclamation of the dead, critics have tended to play down the significance of the exorcism and the epilogue and focus on the ecstatic monologues of the three women of 124. Even Homi Bhabha, whom one would expect to be alert to Morrison's critique of historicism, refers to this section as "a fugue-like ceremony of claiming and naming" in which "it is impossible not to see . . . the healing of a history, a community reclaimed in the making of a name" (17). What Bhabha reads as the celebration of an "interpersonal reality" is in fact a moment of crisis in which Sethe and Denver are sucked into the vortex of Beloved's namelessness. Bhabha fails to recognize that Morrison presents these passages as a *regression* into the narcissism of mother-child relations, a movement that cuts the women of 124 off from the outside world and leads them to *renounce* the need for community and even the need for remembrance. Sethe deludes herself that her daughter's return is a sign that she "was right all along: there is no world outside my door" (185) and that she "don't have to remember nothing" (183).

At stake here is the relationship between subjectivity and community. What Bhabha misrecognizes as the articulation of an "interpersonal reality" is in fact the disarticulation of personality, the dissolution of the individual within the namelessness of the disremembered. The processes of "claiming and naming" that Bhabha rhymes together are in fact radically at odds here: as the women claim each other, their proper names are elided; in assuming a name that is anything but a proper name, they assume Beloved's nonidentity. What Bhabha reads as a healing process of reclaiming the dead is in fact a life-threatening process of being claimed *by* the dead.

Jean Wyatt is much more aware of the life-threatening implications of this dissolution of difference and she shows convincingly how Sethe's inability to metaphorize leads to this regression into the preoedipal symbiosis of mother and daughter. However, her recognition of Sethe's problem with language is at odds with her affirmation of Morrison's own body language. Her argument hinges on lines such as "What she knew was that the responsibility for her breasts was in someone else's hands" (*Beloved* 18), in which "metaphors abandon their symbolic dimension to adhere to a baseline of literal meaning" (475). In this case the metaphor is literalized by the fact that Paul D is physically cupping her breasts. However, Wyatt is reluctant to note what the trajectory of the narrative itself teaches us: that an inability to metaphorize indicates an inability to come to terms with absence and loss, that in order to come to terms with their slave-pasts, the characters must learn to *(re)metaphorize* their bodies. In order to distance themselves from a history of objectification, they need to conceive of themselves as something more than "flesh." If slavery reduced their sexuality to the bodily fact of biological difference, in order to become sexed *subjects* they need to move beyond this crude essentialization of their sexuality and reopen the question of what it means to be a man or a woman in symbolic or sociocultural terms.

Sethe's body language is a direct consequence of the abuse her body has received at the hands of schoolteacher and his "pupils;" it is the unspeakable memory of the way in which her breasts were milked that assigns them their materiality. Her breasts—and by extension, her milk and her children—are that which cannot be lost or mourned, that which resists substitution. Sethe's husband Halle, who witnesses the milking of her breasts, indicates the intolerable nature of Sethe's loss by "smearing butter all over his face" (70). When Paul D tells Sethe of this, Sethe immediately understands that "the milk they took [was] on his mind" (70). As in the examples that Wyatt chooses, Sethe's locution indicates a reduction of metaphor to a baseline of literal meaning: the abstract state of being "on his mind" is reduced to the bodily state of being "all over his face." Halle physically enacts his unbearable proximity to—his inability to distance himself from—the abuse of his wife's body. The only Sweet Home slave to learn to read and write English is reduced to body language as a way of bearing witness to that which he was not able to witness and remain sane. He retreats into a second childhood, an antimetaphorical world of presence and bodily connection, as a way of indicating his inability to countenance Sethe's loss. Like the silent rites of melancholia enacted by Coetzee's figures of alterity, Halle's body language reveals an inability to move beyond the site of an unspeakable loss, an inability to verbalize his grief.

Coetzee's novels explore the impossibility of participating in the other's grief across the divide that separates the privileged from the oppressed; the Magistrate caresses the barbarian girl without being able to enter into her world of suffering. Harris's work explicitly bridges this divide: in caressing Mariella's stripes, the Dreamer is able to enter into her suffering. Morrison explores the problems involved in bearing witness from the perspective of the fellow-oppressed, the impossibility of gaining distance on that which happens to one's own kind. A number of characters attempt to bear belated witness to that which Sethe's husband was not able to witness at the time of its occurrence by describing Sethe's scars as a "chokecherry tree" (79), "roses of blood" (73), and a "sculpture" (19). Freeman reads these descriptions as a mode of aestheticizing the sublime, a redemptive way of speaking about the unspeakable. When Paul D rubs his cheek along "the sculpture her back had become" in order to "learn that way the root of his sorrow" (17), Sethe wonders if she might now be able "to feel the hurt her back ought to" (18), which would indicate that Paul D will function as Dori Laub's empathic witness. Taking up the position that Halle was not able to take up, Paul D seems to offer Sethe the chance to "abreact" her traumatic past. But Freeman fails to give adequate weight to the way in which Sethe's scars resist Paul D's attempt to transfigure them and reassert their brute materiality. Reappraising Sethe's body after a bout of unsatisfactory lovemaking, Paul D comes to see that "the wrought-iron maze he had explored in the kitchen like a gold-miner pawing through pay dirt was in fact a revolting clump of scars" (21). Her scars may in fact be closer to the barbarian girl's indecipherable marks than Mariella's redemptive stripes. Their uncertain status reflects Morrison's own uncertainty about whether it is possible to symbolize and thus mourn the material suffering of slavery.

ALTERNATIVE VERSIONS OF MOTHER LOVE

Morrison's critics have tended to affirm the connection between motherhood and memory in much the same way as they have affirmed the connection between memory and the body. Marianne Hirsch, for instance, celebrates Sethe's "maternal rememory" as "a ground of resistance and opposition" (96), an expression that blurs the distinction between political and psychological modes of resistance, between her attempt to resist being taken back into slavery and her subsequent attempts to "[keep] the past at bay" (42). Sethe's rememory is in fact not simply an *act* of resistance but also the passive, involuntary repetition of an "original" violation—not only Schoolmaster's invasion of 124 but also the initial "theft of the body," of Sethe's maternal rights, that licenses Schoolmaster's invasion. Her inability to believe in time is simultaneously an acknowledgment and a denial of this prior theft. On the one hand, it is a logical response to the precultural position to which she finds herself relegated even on the free side of the Ohio. Because she still lacks the essential rights of white subjects, it is never safe to "go ahead *and count on something*" (38). On the other, it is the sign of a psychic resistance, an inability to come to terms with her vulnerability, an inability to acknowledge that her attempt to put her "babies where they'd be safe . . . didn't work" (164).

Morrison deliberately contrasts Sethe's inability/refusal to accept loss with Baby Suggs's attempt to teach her congregation of escaped slaves how to "cry . . . for the living and the dead" (88). Sethe and Baby Suggs represent two very different reactions to the way in which, in the words of Frederick Douglass, slavery attempted to "blunt and destroy the natural affection of the mother for the child" (qtd. in Spillers 75). Baby Suggs reacts to the loss of all her children by diverting her love outward toward the community, toward the larger, dispersed black "family" that arises in the wake of the dispersal of the biological family of the slave (Spillers 75). It is Baby Suggs—and not, as Wyatt argues, Sethe (and Denver)—who attempts to institute a "maternal symbolic," a "mother love" that, unlike Sethe's, has at its heart an acceptance of dispersal and loss.[11] Recognizing that slavery reduces the captive body to flesh, Baby Suggs urges her congregation to reclaim their bodies, to resubjectivize that which has been reduced to an object, by learning to "love [their] flesh" (88).

If Baby Suggs attempts to resymbolize the body, to make it function once more as the sign of the human, Sethe's relationship to the body and to language moves in precisely the opposite direction, away from the human and toward the inhuman. Unlike Baby Suggs, Sethe refuses to acknowledge the loss of her children, refuses to acknowledge that the social system of slavery cancels her natural right to the ownership of her own offspring. This movement away from the sociocultural reality leads Sethe into a form of biological essentialism in which her motherhood becomes the exclusive sign of her identity. Her overdetermination of herself as a kind of supermother drives her heroic escape from slavery: having sent her children on ahead of her, she knows only that she must escape in order to give them her milk. For Sethe, as Wyatt puts it, "there are no substitutes, metaphorical or otherwise, for her breasts" (478). And it is precisely this refusal to countenance separation that allows her to collect "all the *parts of her* that were precious and fine and beautiful and carr[y], push[ ], drag[ ] them through the veil, out, away, over there where no one could hurt them . . . where they would be safe" (163; emphasis added). Sethe describes her attempt to make her children safe as a mode of birthing in reverse, an attempt to force her children back into the womb.[12] Beloved's return leads Sethe to believe that "the world is in this room" (183) and confirms this movement away from the social by locking 124 into the claustrophobic and seemingly self-sufficient space-time of the womb.

Nevertheless, while making it clear that Baby Suggs's dispersed form of loving is preferable to Sethe's "too-thick" mother love (164), Morrison also makes it clear that, like Baby Suggs, she is unable either "to approve or condemn Sethe's rough choice" to take her children's lives (*Beloved* 180). As Morrison notes, "it was the right thing to do, but she had no right to do it" (Moyers 272). For Baby Suggs, Sethe's act is such a problematic expression of mother love that she gives up preaching. The violation involved in the fact that "they came in her backyard anyway" (180) seems to render futile her injunction to "love thy flesh." Both Schoolmaster's invasion and Sethe's response negate Baby Suggs's attempt to reclaim and resubjectivize the black body. Her efforts to liberate a community of ex-slaves from their history is disrupted by an act of (self-)destruction that suggests the return of racial memory.

RACIAL MEMORY

When Paul D finds out about Sethe's act of infanticide, he "confirms" Schoolteacher's identification of her animal characteristics by reminding her that she's "got two legs, not four" (165), as if he too sees Sethe's act as a regression into animality. His own repetition of the original racist identification is as much a manifestation of racial memory as Sethe's own act; both are symptoms of the unaccommodatable racial memory that Morrison describes as the "jungle whitefolks planted":

> In addition to having to use their heads to get ahead they had the weight of the whole race sitting there. You needed two heads for that. White-people believed that whatever the manners, under every dark skin was a jungle. . . . The more coloredpeople spent their strength trying to convince [whites] how gentle they were, how clever and loving, the more

they used themselves up to persuade whites of something that Negroes believed could not be questioned, the deeper and more tangled the jungle grew inside. But it wasn't the jungle black folks brought with them to this place from the other (liveable) place. It was the jungle whitefolks planted in them. (199)

The black community is unable to forgive Sethe precisely because her infanticide seems to testify to the jungle that "whitefolks" see lurking "under every dark skin," to provide evidence for the racist genetic theory in which blackness is taken to be the sign of a less evolved species, the sign of a genetic predisposition to revert to animal behavior. Morrison plants the seeds of this interpretation early on in the novel, when she tells us that Sethe "did not look away" when " a sow began eating her own litter" (13). However, the passage quoted above subtly dismantles the biological theory by suggesting that the jungle that lodges itself in the flesh of "black folks" is *culturally* produced insofar as it is "planted by whitefolks." The idea of a manmade, cultivated jungle suggests the same conflation of culture and nature that is at the heart of the logic of the symptom, that sign of cultural dis-ease that manifests itself as a biological disorder. Underneath the dark skin that is the biological signifier of race lurks the racial memory of having been identified as less than human, a memory that lodges itself in the flesh precisely because it is a memory of having been reduced to flesh.

HISTORICITY AND THE REAL MOTHER

Although Sethe's act is not the result of a genetic predisposition, it underlies the way in which racial memory functions *as if* it were a biological inheritance, *as if* it were something passed down from generation to generation along with the genes that determine one's physical appearance. Although Sethe's act is an attempt to gain a measure of control over her family's destiny—a way of saying "'I'm a human being. These are my children. This is my script I am writing'" (Morrison in McKay 272)—it is also a manifestation of a collective repetition compulsion, a way of inheriting her mother's own act of defiance.

If Baby Suggs's version of mother love asserts the horizontal cultural ties of the dispersed family, Sethe's mother love attempts to assert the vertical ties of blood kinship, to assert continuity in the face of the discontinuity engendered by slavery. The fierce perversity of this desire (a desire that does indeed reveal an aversion to the *nom du père*, that linguistic marker of both cultural inheritance and bodily separation) is caught in "small-girl" Sethe's desire to be physically marked in the same way as her mother: what Sethe takes as a sign of her mother's singularity is in fact precisely that which denies it: Sethe asks

her mother to "mark the mark on me too" (61) in order to establish lineage
and inheritance, unaware that the brand marks the economic relation that dis-
connects her from her mother and severs the blood tie. Sethe asks for a bodily marker of family as a replacement for the verbal marker, the family name,
that she is denied under slavery.

However, when she gets "a mark of her own" (61) at the hands of
Schoolmaster and his pupils, this mark serves to identify her not with her
mother but with her mother's *defacement*, with the way in which her mother
has literally been rendered unrecognizable after she has been caught trying to
escape: "by the time they cut her down nobody could tell whether she had a
circle and cross or not, least of all me, and I did look" (61). Sethe's own scars
establish a material identity between her and her mother, not as mother and
daughter but as brutalized bodies, common "flesh," "that zero-degree of social
conceptualization" (Spillers 67).

Sethe attempts to define herself against her own mother's failure to be
a mother, her failure to challenge the slave law of discontinuity. Like Michael
K, she devotes herself to a life of nurturing in homage to the mother she never
knew, in order to reestablish the severed connection. Her desire to get her
milk to her children is secretly powered by the fact that her mother, forced to
work in the field, had to give her up to a wet nurse. Similarly, her refusal to
contemplate escaping without her children is haunted by the suspicion that
her own mother tried to escape without her (203). Nevertheless, despite her
best intentions, she ends up repeating her mother's actions, first by giving
birth in a boat, and second by her act of infanticide. Sethe inadvertently consigns Beloved to the same "nameless place" as her mother consigned her own
babies. Repeatedly raped by the crew during the Middle Passage, Sethe's
mother threw her unwanted babies overboard: "without names, she threw
them" (107). Ultimately, then, Sethe's act of resistance is not an act of self-def-
inition but rather an erasure of her own subjectivity and singularity: her own
identity is swallowed up as she becomes one in a long line of mothers who
responded in the same way to the intolerable "contradiction of mothering
under slavery" (Wyatt 476). Their "unnatural," "inhuman" violence has its origin in the prior violence against nature and humanity, the institution of slavery itself.

Sethe's act of infanticide loses its historical specificity at precisely the
point at which it intersects with the act of a real historical woman. Mae Henderson takes the fact that *Beloved* was inspired by a newspaper clipping about
a woman named Margaret Garner,[13] who also attempted to kill her children
rather than let them be taken back into slavery, as a sign that Morrison both
"historicizes fiction and fictionalizes history" (64). For Henderson, the newspaper clipping functions to locate the novel within history and to turn it into
a form of cultural memory. However the clipping in fact functions to *dis*locate

both novel and history, to locate both within the traumatic, repetitious time of racial memory. By building her narrative around an act of infanticide, Morrison is not so much filling in the gaps in the historical archive as indicating the presence of an unhistoricizable event, one that opens up a breach within historical time.

To put it another way, Morrison's novel is most realistic, most faithful to history, at precisely the same moment that it is most fantastic. This is the double valency with which Lacan invests the Real in order to indicate an order of existence that is more real than reality insofar as it is structured by our most primal or prehistoric fantasies. One of the most enduring of these "pre-historic" fantasies is of a mother who devours her own children, the mythical and terrible figure that psychoanalysis refers to as the Real or primal mother.[14] While Sethe's mother throws her children overboard as a mode of disowning the children fathered by whites, Sethe murders Beloved as a way of asserting her ownership rights over children fathered by the man whom she claims—despite her inability, as a slave, to legalize their union— as her husband. While Sethe's mother's actions are a bitter confirmation of the severance of blood ties under slavery, Sethe's act is an attempt to deny this law of severance by picking up those whom she conceives of as "parts of herself" and putting them "where they'd be safe." Even the syntax of her thought—a syntax that will later characterize Beloved's own thought—is a denial of severance. When Sethe catches sight of Schoolteacher's hat and flees to the outhouse, "if she thinks anything it is No. Nono. Nonono" (106). However, because she can only preempt the Law by taking a handsaw to her child's throat, she inadvertently herself becomes the Law of severance, condemning her child to an eternity of "want[ing] to join" (213). In taking the Law into their own hands, both Sethe and her mother partake in the transgressive enjoyment or *jouissance* of the Real mother.[15] But in so doing, they separate themselves not only from their children but also from themselves. In taking on the identity of the Real Mother, they forfeit their identities as ordinary mothers. In assuming the proportions of myth, their actions lose their specificity.

Sethe is only able to tell Denver, and Denver only wants to hear about, the creative side of this mythic identity. Sethe tells and retells Denver the "told story" (29) of the pregnant supermother who escaped slavery in order to get her milk to her children. But she cannot tell her about the destructive side of her resistance to slavery, the untellable story of the mother who cuts her babies' throats. And yet this untellable story is nevertheless passed on: Sethe returns in Denver's "monstrous and unmanageable dreams" (103) in which Sethe cuts Denver's head off and carries it downstairs in order to comb and braid her hair. Along with stories of milk, Sethe also inadvertently suckles Denver with stories of blood. Indeed, despite Baby Suggs's attempts to prevent her, Sethe literally suckles Denver when her breasts are still bloody after cutting Beloved's throat (152). It is precisely because she has already secretly received this untellable story of her mother's Real identity that Denver abandons school and turns stone deaf when Nelson Lord poses "the question about her mother" (102). Some stories are only transmissible as symptom.

In her analysis of this "fantastic" recurrence of the Real Mother, Helene Moglen argues that Morrison "lifts the primal mother out of that prelinguistic space [of the Real] and returns her to history" (22). While Moglen is right to suggest that Morrison historicizes psychoanalysis by showing how the mythical figure has an "origin" in an actual history, I would argue that Morrison also reveals the limits of historicism by showing how some experiences are only recordable, only transmissible, as myth. Morrison's attempt to tell the story of her "tribe" assumes mythic proportions at precisely the point where the story becomes unspeakable, at precisely the point where the tellable cultural memory collapses into the untellable racial memory.

SPEAKING THE UNSPEAKABLE?

Henderson's historicist reading assumes that it is Morrison's role to speak the unspeakable. What Henderson misses is the way in which Morrison structures her novel in order to suggest the inaccessibility of certain orders of experience. She fails to note that the primary subject of the narrative is not slavery itself but the problem of remembering slavery: Morrison deliberately sets the novel in the era of Reconstruction, on the free side of the Ohio, as if to announce a limit to her imaginative freedom as a novelist to enter into the consciousness of a slave. In so doing, Morrison aligns her own task as novelist with Sethe's problem in remembering Sweet Home; Sethe's shame at being able to remember "the most beautiful sycamores in the world" (6) but not the bodies that hung from them is also Morrison's. And if slavery is only presentable as a series of disorienting flashbacks,[16] the Middle Passage is even less available to representation. Morrison underlines the impossibility of recalling the experience of what it was like to be on the slave ships by incorporating them within the memory of someone who, to borrow Sethe's description of Denver, "was never there" (36).

Henderson's argument is supported by some of Morrison's own comments about her work. In "Site of Memory," for instance, Morrison seems to recognize no limits to her imaginative freedom, characterizing herself as recovering the "interior life" of the slave that the slave narratives left out, and "rip[ping] the veil drawn over proceedings too terrible to relate" (110–12; also qtd. in Henderson 63). However, Morrison's key critical essay, "Unspeakable

Things Unspoken: The Afro-American Presence in American Literature,"[17] delivered the year after the publication of *Beloved,* demonstrates a more complex understanding of her literary endeavor, one that parallels the ambiguity which Matus detects in Morrison's approach to memorialization. The essay moves from an examination of how race functions as an *aporia* within the white imagination to a discussion of how race functions in her own novels. At first glance, the implied logic of this shift is that her own novels give voice to that which remains unspoken in white American literature. Morrison's gloss on the opening sentences of her first novel, *The Bluest Eye,* which relate a break in the natural order (the nonappearance of marigolds) to the fact that Pecola is carrying her father's child, seems to support this logic. According to Morrison, the opening sentence "provides the stroke that announces something more than a secret shared, but a silence broken, a void filled, *an unspeakable thing spoken at last*" (20; emphasis added). However, it is important to note that it is Cholly's rape of his own daughter, and not Cholly's own "rape" at the hands of white men, that is spoken at last. The "primal" scene of racial abuse that secretly determines the implosion of the Breedlove family remains undisclosed.

Indeed, as Morrison begins to approach the subject of race more directly, the historicist paradigm of a recovered presence is completely abandoned. In the very next paragraph of the lecture, Morrison says:

> [A] problem lies in the central chamber of the novel. The shattered world I built (to complement what is happening to Pecola) . . . does not in its present form handle effectively the silence at its center: the void that is Pecola's "unbeing." It should have had a shape—like the emptiness left by a boom or a cry. (22)

The Bluest Eye, Morrison seems to be arguing here, fails to do Pecola justice precisely by representing her too much, by failing to indicate her lack of presence, her unbeing. In one paragraph Morrison conceives of herself as filling a void and breaking a silence; in the next, she takes herself to task for failing to construct a void, for failing to leave room for a silence. At one moment she speaks of the need for remembrance and recovery, at another of the need to indicate what cannot be remembered or recovered.

In the next paragraph, Morrison signals her awareness of this contradiction by describing her work as the attempt "to shape a silence while breaking it" (23). My distinction between cultural and racial memory is my attempt to name this seemingly contradictory double movement. On the one hand, Morrison is clearly in the business of reclaiming an African American cultural history and subjectivity; her novels are a way of redressing the representational bias of American literature and affording the black community both aesthetic and political representation. On the other, she wants to indi-

cate the negating effect of racism, the way in which racism disallows subjectivity and "dirt̶y̶ ̶ ̶ ̶ ̶ ̶ ̶ ̶ ̶ ̶ ̶ ̶ ̶you forgot who you were and couldn't think it up"
̶ ̶ ̶ ̶ ̶ ̶ ̶ ̶ ̶ ̶ ̶ ̶ ̶ ̶ ̶process of mourning and working through by
̶ ̶ ̶ ̶ ̶ ̶ ̶ ̶ ̶ ̶ ̶ ̶ ̶eks to "shape a silence" in order to indicate a

̶ ̶ ̶ ̶ ̶ ̶ ̶ ̶ ̶ ̶ as M̶o̶r̶r̶ison argues, as the "ghost in the machine" of
̶ ̶ ̶ ̶ ̶ ̶s̶p̶e̶a̶k̶a̶b̶le" l3), this presence becomes literalized as a
̶ ̶ ̶ ̶ ̶ ̶al. This p̶r̶o̶cess of literalization is not a rendering speak-
̶ ̶ ̶ ̶ ̶able) but a̶n̶ indication of the presence of that which, *even
̶ ̶ ̶ ̶on an african American text*, remains unspeakable. Morrison achieves in
̶B̶eloved pr̶e̶c̶i̶s̶ely what she fails to achieve in *The Bluest Eye*, by incorporating
̶ ̶into th̶e̶ narr̶ative a subject who is not a subject, a ghost whose "unbeing"
̶s̶t̶r̶uctur̶es a̶ silence that bears witness to that which cannot be mourned. At
t̶h̶e cent̶er of what is, after all, a cultural text, Morrison places an inner cham-
b̶e̶r̶ that̶ functions as an empty tomb or crypt, as a way of remembering those
w̶h̶o̶m the novel is unable to lay to rest. And it is only by so doing that the
n̶o̶vel i̶s able to achieve its work of mourning. To restate my initial thesis, it is
o̶n̶ly by recognizing the excessive nature of collective history, by assigning a
l̶i̶m̶it to the work of mourning, that the racially marked are able to come to
t̶e̶rms with their personal histories.

AN INJUNCTION TO REMEMBER

Toward the end of the novel, Paul D asks Denver whether Beloved "sure
'nough [her] sister" (266). Denver replies: "At times I think she was more" as
if in tacit reference to "the Sixty Million and more" of the novel's epigraph.
Paul D himself tells Stamp Paid that Beloved "reminds [him] of something.
Something, look like, I'm supposed to remember" (234), something that lies
just outside memory's reach but which nonetheless never ceases to exert a certain pressure, a certain demand, for remembrance. Beloved functions not as
that which must be remembered but as that which, by indicating the collective history that cannot be mourned, marks off the personal history that can
be mourned. She functions as what one might call a catalyst for remembrance:
while her own immemorial state remains fundamentally unchanged throughout the novel, her presence allows the living to begin to come to terms with
their own pasts.

Beloved's presence as the materialization of racial memory ultimately
allows Sethe and Paul D to dematerialize their own pasts. Although on a first
reading it seems as if Beloved is precisely what comes between Paul D and
Sethe and prevents them from making a family, her intervention is in fact
what enables them finally to come together. Before her arrival, it seems as if

Paul D and Sethe will be able to provide a mutual holding space that will allow them both to come to terms with their respective pasts. Paul D tells Sethe, "Go as far inside as you need to, I'll hold your ankles" (46). However, as soon as he finds out about her past and reminds her of how many legs she has, Morrison tells us that "a forest sprang up between them; trackless and quiet" (165). This forest is a close relation of the "jungle that whitefolks planted in them" (198). Before Sethe and Paul D can come together, they need to distance themselves from the memory of the reduction of their bodies to animal flesh. Paul D later wonders whether it was the memory of having been forced to sodomize calves that inspired his insult. Before he can return to 124 and "place his *story* next to hers" (273, emphasis added), both of them need to rehumanize, to dematerialize and remetaphorize, their bodies. Unlike Sethe's expression of her love for her children, Paul D's final expression of his love for Sethe *reverses* the process of literalization, turning the physical act of laying his body down beside hers into a metaphor. Like the turtles that Denver watches making love, whose clashing shells mock their attempts at greater intimacy (105), Sethe and Paul D are unable to come together until they have transformed the bodily weight of their respective pasts into the symbolic, verbal form of stories.

In order to dematerialize their own histories, both Sethe and Paul D need to relinquish the overliteral—"overbodily"—sexual identities that they have developed in response to slavery's denial of their sexual rights and learn to understand their sexuality—especially the "fact" of their "castration"—in metaphorical, sociocultural, terms. As we shall see, Beloved plays a crucial role in this process.

Documenting His Manhood

Beloved seduces Paul D in the hope that he will "touch [her] in [her] inside part and call [her] by [her] name" (116). While Paul D's saying of her name fails to satisfy her need for remembrance and love, it escorts Paul D "to some ocean-deep place he once belonged to" (264). This encounter with the immemorial aspect of his collective history enables him to confront that which is unspeakable in his own history: when he reaches Beloved's "inside part," instead of saying her name he is shouting "red heart, red heart," absorbed by the way in which she has blown open his "rusty tobacco tin" (117) and released the memories of slavery that he has attempted to keep internally sealed off. Wyatt notes the literality of the way in which Beloved "moves" Paul D out of 124 and into the church cellar, but fails to note the way in which the scene of seduction *reengages the metaphorical level* and "moves" Paul D emotionally, allowing him to mourn his own past.

While their lovemaking proves Paul D's literal potency (he makes her pregnant), it also confirms his metaphorical impotence or powerlessness: she reduces him to the status of a "rag doll—picked up and put down anywhere anytime by a girl young enough to be his daughter. Fucking her when he was convinced he didn't want to" (124). In desperation, and unable to tell Sethe "I am not a man," he undertakes to "document his manhood" (128) literally—by making Sethe pregnant. But this reduction of the question of his manhood to the bodily level of biological function is precisely the problem. Only once he has retreated to the church cellar is he able to confront the question of his manhood on a metaphorical or cultural level.

Part of Paul D's problem is that his initial conception of his own manhood was articulated in a language that was not his own—the language of his owner. In the cellar, Paul D recalls how Sweet Home's initial owner, Garner, was proud of having "raised his niggers as men" (220). Allowed to carry guns and speak to Garner man to man, the slaves fail to realize the provisional nature of a manhood that remains dependent on Garner's word. When Garner dies, Schoolteacher arrives and takes away the word by refusing to listen to their advice, by relieving them of their guns, by treating them, in short, as laboring animals. In reducing them to the status of objects in what now reveals itself as an exclusively white man's symbolic, Schoolteacher teaches them that as slaves they are denied the status of men. In the absence of a cultural definition of their manhood, they are forced to identify themselves exclusively in terms of their biological sex.

In order to extricate himself from the white man's symbolic, Paul D needs to articulate his masculinity in nonbodily terms. Until he is able to do this, Paul D is haunted by material or overbodily reminders of the fact of his castration; his penis continually "returns" until he is able to mourn the loss of his manhood in cultural, sociopolitical terms. It returns first in the form of a cock named "Mister." As he is led away from Sweet Home, he catches sight of a rooster whose freedom and physical power counterpoints Paul D's captivity and powerlessness. The bit with which Paul D is hitched to the cart that takes him away from Sweet Home literally impedes his speech, rendering him incapable of verbalizing his humiliation. When he relates this scene to Sethe many years later, he begins to articulate this castration in metaphorical terms, as a question of title and name: "Even if you cooked him you'd be cooking a rooster named Mister. But wasn't no way I'd ever be Paul D again" (72). The rooster's name reminds Paul D of precisely the title to which he is unable to lay claim. His patronym (Garner), which should function to document his manhood and establish the vertical rights of inheritance, serves only to announce the name of his owner, while the letter D serves only to locate him in a horizontal series as one disinherited slave among others. In the cellar, mulling over these and other humiliations, he comes to understand that he was never truly in possession of the name of the father. The syntax with which he verbalizes his castration—"they clipped him, Paul D. First his shot gun, then his thoughts" (220)—reveals the way in which his name is powerless to prevent a castration that had already taken place before Schoolteacher arrived.

However, before he arrives at this understanding of the symbolic nature of his castration, he is forced to act out his castration in bodily terms. After his encounter with the cock, penises continue to assault him in the flesh. Immediately prior to his escape, his warders offer him and his fellow chain-gang members their penises for "breakfast" (107). Immediately after his escape, a woman waives his offer to do her woodpile and feeds him "pork sausage, the worst thing in the world for a starving man" (131). Thus, although he has become "the sort of man who could walk into the house and make the women cry" (17) by the time he arrives at 124, he remains haunted by the need to assert his sexuality. He attempts to exorcise the ghost that haunts 124 by smashing up the interior with a table, a display of manliness that serves only to precipitate Beloved's materialization. It is not until Beloved forces him into a "damp and warm" church cellar—a womblike space which, unlike the earth of his first birthing/liberation, is also a cultural space at the heart of the community—that he experiences his "second" birth. As he emerges from the cellar he meets Stamp Paid, who ferries him to a new level of freedom by helping him to verbalize his political impotence as a black man in Reconstruction America, to rearticulate his castration as a mode of social solidarity: "'Tell me something Stamp . . . how much is a nigger supposed to take?' 'All he can,' said Stamp Paid, 'All he can.' 'Why? Why? Why? Why? Why?'" (235). In reopening the question of his manhood as a political rather than a biological matter, Paul D tentatively begins to articulate what Lacan would describe as "authentic speech," and to announce his belated arrival as a speaking subject.

LAYING IT ALL DOWN

Just before Beloved arrives, Paul D takes Sethe and Denver to a carnival, an act that seems to presage the beginnings of a "liveable" family life: "They were not holding hands but their shadows were" (47). After Paul D is expelled, the three women hold their own private carnival, to celebrate the return of Sethe's daughter, and Sethe concludes that "the hand-holding shadows she had seen on the road were not Paul D, Denver and herself but 'us three'"—the mother and her two daughters (182). Barbara Freeman seemingly agrees with Sethe's conclusion in her assertion that "Beloved is the absent third who is missing from 124" (135), an assertion that is consonant with her emphasis on a mourning that celebrates connection rather than severance but that completely ignores the sinister dramatic irony that Morrison wants us to see in Sethe's celebration of Beloved's return: while Paul D leads Sethe and Denver out of 124 and into the world of the living, Beloved confines them to the house—Sethe eventually gives up her job, and with it, their food supply—and begins to suck them into the world of the dead.

The irony is particularly marked when Sethe decides to take them skating. Unlike the trip to the carnival, this trip is a private one, one that only transports them deeper into the psychic time-space of 124. As they fall over on the ice, Morrison takes up what functions as a refrain for the whole section of the novel: "Nobody saw them falling" (174). As with Beloved's moving of Paul D, the literal meaning of this expression gives way to a metaphorical, emotional meaning: the three are falling for each other, engaged in a kind of free fall that will culminate in the tripartite statement of possession: "You are mine/You are mine/You are mine" (217). Although I argued earlier that this movement constitutes a dissolution of identity, a life-threatening identification with the dead, it is also, like Paul D's coupling with Beloved, a means of becoming reacquainted with "some ocean deep place [they] once belonged to." This obscure encounter with their own prehistory allows them to confront their own pasts, to "lay it all down" (174), as Baby Suggs once preached. However, while Baby Suggs exhorted the community to lay it all down in the Clearing, Sethe lays it all down in the context of a private carnival that moves her further and further away from the community. While Baby Suggs's mourning ritual "clears" a "liveable" space in the jungle of racial memory, Sethe attempts to inhabit the unliveable space of the jungle itself.

The passage in which Morrison speaks of racial memory and the "jungle that white men planted" immediately precedes the women's monologues and is in fact presented as the thoughts of Stamp Paid, as he ponders why he is unable to gain entrance to 124:

> When Sethe locked the door, the women were free at last . . . to say whatever was on their minds.
>   Almost. Mixed in with the voices surrounding the house, recognizable but undecipherable to Stamp Paid, were the thoughts of the women of 124, unspeakable thoughts, unspoken. (199)

The "mumbling of the black and angry dead" (198) thus becomes mixed in with what the women of 124 are unable to articulate about their own lives. As 124 attempts to accommodate that which cannot be accommodated, it turns itself from a womb into a tomb, a cryptic space of "undecipherable" language. The monologues that follow thus do not constitute a speaking of the unspeakable. The very fact that they are *interior* monologues suggests that the thoughts of the women of 124 remain unspoken. The first three monologues are pointedly *not* addressed to the other women: they refer to the other women in the third person and articulate personal histories that remain unshared. In the last section or "polylogue," the women do finally seem to be communicating with one another, as if they shared the same interior space. That this is cause for alarm rather than celebration is made clear once again by means of dramatic irony: Sethe begins to confuse Baby Suggs's injunction to lay it all down with her final lying down, her communal ritual of remembrance with her abandoning of her role of preacher and her lying down to die.[18] In order to block out the world and its pain, Baby Suggs determines only to "think about the color of things" (177), rigorously resisting the metaphorical, political implications of this phrase (the injustice of racism) by focusing exclusively on the yellow patches on her quilt. In her monologue, Sethe recalls Baby Suggs's fixation on color: "Now I know why Baby Suggs pondered color her last years. She never had time to see, let alone enjoy it before" (201). What Sethe takes to be a revelation of how to enjoy life is in fact a mode of retreating from life, a mode of preparing oneself for death. As Sethe herself puts it, "Now I can sleep *like the drowned*" (204; emphasis added). To lay it all down is ultimately to give up the burden of remembrance, to succumb to the oblivion of those who drowned during the Middle Passage.

EXORCISM

Ella, the woman who heads the exorcism party, is a lot less ambiguous than Morrison's critics about the significance of Beloved's return: while "she didn't mind a little communication between the two worlds," for a ghost to take on flesh constituted "an invasion" (257). When the women begin to keen, for Sethe it is as if the Clearing has come to 124: unlike Sethe's body language, this communal act of maternal lamentation seeks not only to "break the back of words" but also to sever the melancholic bond that ties Sethe to Beloved and imprisons her within the asocial, atemporal time-space of 124. This process of severance is completed with the reappearance of the "third term," of that which conventionally breaks the symbiosis of mother and child, in the form of a hat that Sethe takes to be schoolteacher's. This time around, instead of retreating into the cold house to take her children's lives, she runs towards the perceived threat, simultaneously stepping out of the "told story" of 124 and separating herself from Beloved.

A BREATHING SPACE

Only after Beloved's exorcism is there space for Paul D's desire; her departure makes possible his return. Sethe's house is no longer an impossible space of maternal presence, but merely a house from which Paul D senses that something is missing. He feels "an absence" as he passes through the door, and Sethe's bed "seems to him a place where he is not" (270). Sethe's "exhausted breasts" indicate that she can no longer define herself as a maternal body, while his own offer to bathe her—traditionally a maternal role, and something that Baby Suggs did for Sethe upon her arrival at 124—signals that his overriding concern is no longer to document his manhood.

It seems that they can only come together as man and woman once they have relinquished their overessentialized sexual identities. Sethe verbalizes her loss and thus acknowledges her "lack" as a mother with the words "she left me" (272). After all the invasions of the novel, his desire "to put his story next to hers" is scrupulously noninvasive, anxious not to rematerialize a personal history that can finally be laid to rest. Looking at Sethe, Paul D recalls Sixo's description of his relation to the thirty mile woman: "She is a friend of my mind. She gather me, man" (273). What Sethe's presence does for Paul D, Paul D's words do for Sethe: in answer to her cry that "[Beloved] was [her] best thing" (272) he tells her "you your best thing, Sethe, you are" (273). His position of alterity—unlike Beloved's position of identity—allows her to see herself from the outside, and, like Paul D on the church steps, she is finally able to articulate her subjecthood with the repetition of a question: "Me? Me?" (273).

EPILOGUE: THE NEGATIVE GROUND OF RACIAL IDENTITY

While personal histories can be laid to rest, the collective history to which Beloved has attempted to give voice remains "a loneliness that roams" (274). Her story, Morrison tells us, "was not a story to pass on" (274). For Henderson, this enigmatic pronouncement—which she takes to refer to the novel as a whole and not just Beloved's story—must be explained away: "If we were to take this injunction seriously, how then can we explain Morrison's commitment to a project of recovery and 'rememory?' Clearly such an injunction would threaten to contradict the motive and sense of the entire novel" (83). Henderson solves this problem by suggesting that "what the narrator must mean" is not that "the novel is NOT a story to 'be passed on'" (retold) but rather that it is "not a story to be PASSED ON," not a story we can ignore.

However, I would argue that the first sense of the phrase remains primary: Beloved's story, the story of the Sixty Million and more, is not a verbally transmissible story. While Morrison passes on to us the tellable story of Sethe's and Paul D's mourning, she also encrypts within this tellable story the untellable, unmournable story of the Middle Passage. This cryptic story is passed on to us as that which refuses to pass on, that which can never be laid to rest precisely because it can never be adequately told. As Jean Wyatt puts it, Beloved's story "continues to haunt the borders of a symbolic order that excludes it" (484).

Like Coetzee's *Foe, Beloved* gestures beyond its own discursive limits in order to indicate a history that it has not been able to remember or recover. Like Friday, Beloved must remain "disremembered" (274). Barbara Freeman suggests that "[a]s the signifier of absence, Beloved allows both characters and readers a point of entry to that which has been absent in our history" (137). In fact, this is exactly what both Beloved and Friday *dis*allow: they mark the limits of our ability to empathize and identify, the impossibility of putting ourselves in the shoes of those who were reduced to the status of flesh. Morrison's after-text thus seems closer to Coetzee's antiredemptive vision than to Harris's vision of redemption. While for Harris no soul lies beyond redemption, both Morrison and Coetzee are forced to acknowledge the existence of lonely, "disremembered" souls/bodies that lie beyond the embrace of their respective narratives. Unlike the intersubjective communion that ends *Palace of the Peacock,* both *Foe* and *Beloved* end with a lonely vision of noncommunion.

However, while Coetzee's recognition of a limit to the work of mourning leaves his narratives inconsolable, Morrison's recognition of a similar limit enables a work of mourning to take place at the level of the individual. Like the Dreamer, Beloved functions as a catalyst for remembrance. Just as the Dreamer enables Donne to recognize his own guilt as a colonizer in *Palace of the Peacock,* Beloved allows a family of escaped slaves to come to terms with the guilt of having survived, to negotiate the claims of those who did not make it, those whom they have been forced to leave behind. It is as if the survival of Sethe, Paul D, and even Denver is predicated on the recognition of those who did not survive, as if their movement toward "some kind of tomorrow" is dependent on recognizing those who remain in limbo, as if the realization of their own subjecthood is bound up with the remembrance of the subjectless anonymity of the Sixty Million and more.

Morrison finds a way of transforming the oppressive weight of racial memory, "the weight of the whole race sitting there," into an affirmation of "some ocean deep place they once belonged to." But this affirmation is crucially not an affirmation of belonging—the desire to belong again to such a place is, as we have seen, a form of death wish—but an affirmation of having *once* belonged. And it is not Africa that is affirmed as the place to which they once belonged, but the oceanic space of the Middle Passage, the space of departure without arrival to which it is impossible to belong. Like Harris, Morrison recognizes the impossibility of reclaiming an African tradition and turns this impossibility into the ground of a new possibility. For it is precisely the strange, negative "affirmation" of a lost origin, of an original, unmournable loss, that enables Morrison's characters to contemplate the future. In the final instance, *Beloved* asks us to reconceive of racial identity and community as grounded not in the continuous history of cultural tradition but rather in the discontinuous history of racial trauma.

SOME KIND OF COMMUNITY

What the state cannot tolerate in any way . . . is that the singularities
form a community without affirming identity, that humans co-belong
without any representable condition of belonging (86).
            —Giorgio Agamben, *The Coming Community*

I began by asking whether it was possible to found community on a recognition of our infinite difference. Giorgio Agamben's dream of a community
that would not be dependent on the affirmation of identity or sameness is
echoed by Jean-Luc Nancy's vision of a "community of others," a community
perhaps only truly realizable in death: "Community is what takes place always
through others and for others. . . . If community is revealed in the death of
others it is because death itself is the true community of others" (15). Community is the impossible destination of postcolonial narrative, signaled not
only by Harris's celebratory vision of communion at the end of *Palace of the
Peacock* but also by the lonely after-texts at the end of *Foe* and *Beloved*, which
provide negative images of the coming community, gesturing toward the
need for a more inclusive collectivity by indicating what still remains
excluded. Harris's vision of community is a presentiment or promise rather
than a fully realized representation or resolution, a promise that must be infinitely renewed. Like mourning, the attempt to redraw the boundaries of
community must remain incomplete, unsuccessful; its success is measured
precisely by its failure to complete itself, its capacity to remain perpetually
open to the difference of the other, to the possibility of different others and
not yet imagined modes of being.

111

In 1992, Stuart Hall announced "the end of the innocent notion of the essential black subject" (443), a demise brought about by "the recognition that 'black' is essentially a politically and culturally constructed category which cannot be grounded in a set of fixed trans-cultural or transcendental racial categories and which therefore has no guarantees in nature" (443). Hall proposes that we understand blackness as a cultural rather than a biological category, as an ethnicity rather than a race, although he warns that the term ethnicity must be "dis-articulated from its position in the discourse of multi-culturalism" where it is often used as a means of "disavowing the realities of racism" (446). He calls for an "ethnicity of the margins . . . a recognition that we all speak from a particular place, out of a particular history, out of a particular experience, a particular culture, without being contained by that position. . . . We are all, in that sense, *ethnically* located and our ethnic identities are crucial to our subjective sense of who we are" (447).

Like many other formulations of cultural difference, Hall's redefinition of ethnicity risks losing sight of the realities of racism because it assumes that we are all able "to speak from a particular place," that there is no place from which it is impossible to enter into the cultural conversation. It loses sight of those bodies that acquire a certain materiality precisely because they have been denied access to the discursive realm of culture. So called antiessentialist theories of the subject that emphasize the provisional and constantly shifting parameters of identity fail to account for this extradiscursive materiality of the racially marked body. I have argued for an antihistoricist ethics of remembrance in an attempt to show how the racially marked body is never fully identifiable; like Fanon and Spivak's excessive, hemorrhaging corpses, it is never fully locatable in history.

As Charles Shepherdson argues, the body cannot be exclusively accounted for either as a biological or cultural phenomenon, either in terms of sex and race or gender and ethnicity. His argument is similarly directed against the ascendancy of historicism in contemporary debates over culture and identity.

> If we question the limits of historicism, then, we do so not to propose a return to the reality of empirical facts or in the name of biological truth, but because the historicity of various phenomena—what we might call their modes of temporalization—has often been prematurely reduced to a single form by the discourse of social construction. In this sense the body—perhaps like race itself—cannot be adequately grasped if it is regarded as a discursive effect or a purely symbolic formation. (44)

In our desire to move away from genetic theories of race and the vicissitudes of biological essentialism, we have perhaps fallen prey to a form of cultural essentialism in which the subject is the sum of its various culturally and historically determined parts.

Hall refers to Derrida's notion of *différance* as instrumental in bringing about the end of the innocent notion of the black subject but warns "if we are concerned to maintain a politics it cannot be defined exclusively in terms of an infinite sliding of the signifier" (447). Such a drawing back from the perceived irresponsibility of "full-blown" deconstruction/poststructuralism is characteristic of the present era of postcolonial studies, sometimes wishfully labeled "posttheoretical." A true differing or deconstruction of the subject would lead not to pantextualism (as deconstruction's opponents charge) but to the attempt to think community without recourse to the idea of sameness or similitude. What "we" have in common is not the various different cultural affiliations of race, class, gender, sexuality, religion, for these affiliations necessarily produce exclusions as well as overlaps and thus ultimately work against the very idea of community. We need to think beyond the idea of solidarity based on a commonality of interest. What we have in common is simply our "being"—a being that we might learn to think of on the one hand as our embodiedness and on the other as our indebtedness.

To define our being as embodiment is to recognize that we "co-belong" simply as sentient beings. It is this "simple respect for human suffering" (Appiah) that grounds our awareness of injustice and produces a nonexclusionary form of solidarity. The recent work of Derrida and Coetzee has been concerned to expand this ethical universal to include other sentient beings, those who share not Reason but simply the capacity to feel.[1] But this horizontal or spatial definition of our co-belonging needs to be supplemented by a vertical or temporal understanding of being as indebtedness: "That we *are* heirs does not mean that we have or that we receive this or that . . . but that the being of what we are *is* first of all inheritance" (Derrida, *Specters* 54). It should be clear by now that the deconstruction of the subject is not the pastime of privileged Western academics but a powerful way of thinking beyond self-interest and toward an ethics based on our responsibility for and to the other.

The idea of being as inheritance is what links those working within the tradition of deconstruction[2] with diasporic thinkers such as Gilroy, Glissant, and Harris, for whom a history of material and cultural disinheritance means that the very idea of inheritance, the means by which one relates to the past, has to be reinvented. In Gilroy's understanding of the Black Atlantic as a "discursive formation," a nationalist version of essentialism sometimes seems to be replaced by a cross-cultural form of essentialism, a diasporic mode of identification that simply recognizes the transnational scope of black cultural production. However, his emphasis on a melancholic collective memory of the slavery points to the way in which black subjectivity in fact remains not simply dispersed but radically incomplete and inconsolable. The work of Harris and Glissant perhaps goes further than Gilroy's concept of the Black Atlantic in suggesting that we all—both black and white—might learn to inherit this history of disinheritance. For these thinkers the Middle Passage forms an abyss that, like the Holocaust, provides the ethical basis for a truly cross-cultural sense of indebtedness. Being as indebtedness is here indissolubly linked to being as embodiment insofar as what is inherited is a memory of the body in pain.

In bearing witness toward histories of racial oppression that are not entirely recoverable, the work of Coetzee, Harris, and Morrison is characterized by what one might call an aesthetics—or ethics—of incompletion. Their work enables us to acknowledge that which secretly unhinges the self, that which fails to add up to a fully present subject, leaving us with a model of subjectivity in which the self, far from accruing a history and an identity like so much cultural capital, instead comes to an awareness of its infinite obligation toward others. By incorporating history into their narratives as a spectral presence rather than attempting to recover it as a fully narratable subject, they force their readers to reflect critically on the nature of their own engagement with history and alterity. Each narrative brings the reader into relation with a material level of suffering that refuses to be translated into historical discourse. The indigestible nature of this history of suffering is more marked in the work of Coetzee and Morrison, where it is literally spat up into an aftertext. In Harris, suffering is rendered digestible by being transfigured into sacrament. However, because there can be no end to our responsibility, the "morsel cooking in the sun" always remains to be eaten, the ritual of consumption infinitely repeated. And it is with the acknowledgment of this irreducible remainder, this reminder of a history that never ceases to exert a claim but which resists being claimed, that the work of mourning truly begins.

Insofar as the postcolonial work of mourning is addressed to a community that has yet to be formed, it thus constitutes itself as an infinite address. In other words, it refuses to allow us to conceive of ourselves as finite beings; it forces us to conceive of ourselves as infinitely responsible for bringing into being this community. In an attempt to accommodate that which haunts the present, we become noncontemporaneous with ourselves. We come to conceive of identity as "a story with a hole in it" (*Michael K* 110), "nothing" (*Palace of the Peacock* 114), or "more" (*Beloved* 266), three versions of an indebted or "deconstructed" subject whose difference from one another I have endeavored to respect.

In Coetzee's narratives our own existence becomes irrevocably bound up with the suffering of others. Like the Magistrate, we find that "something has fallen in upon [us] from the sky . . . for which [we are] responsible" (*Waiting for the Barbarians* 43). We can no longer block our ears to the sounds coming from the granary. The task here is to place our own subjectivity under erasure, to create a space of silence within the self that might allow "other voices [to] speak in our lives" (*Foe* 30). Although this space only seems to emerge in the dream lives of Coetzee's characters, Coetzee implicitly suggests that the act of reading opens up a similar space insofar as reading is the suspension of what Freud terms our "self-regard" ("Mourning and Melancholia" 252). However, Coetzee is also aware that reading, like dreaming, is the scene of a certain wish fulfillment and may in fact be nothing but the expression of our self-regard. What we think of as an empathic process of identification may well be a narcissistic process of projection, a false exit from the labyrinth of self-consciousness. Nevertheless, Coetzee's novels persist in this attempt to circumnavigate consciousness. Through the holes in his narrators' self-regard, we gain glimpses of the materiality of the other's suffering.

Harris's narratives constitute a more complete relinquishing of self-regard. As the crew travel upriver, they too become aware of other voices in their lives. In the first instance, these voices are the voices of the families that they have fathered and abandoned. But these voices are also the voices of their ancestors, voices that are present in the enigma of the Arawak woman whom they rape in their passage through "the straits of memory" (62), in the silence of a woman who "belonged to a race that neither forgave nor forgot" (61). In a more conventional narrative, these voices of conscience and responsibility would lead to a series of domestic homecomings and to the reestablishment of the patriarchal subject. But in *Palace of the Peacock* these voices signal the dissolution of the finite subject. In the process of discarding their lust to rule, each discovers that he is "nothing in himself" (114).

In *Beloved*, the excessive memory of the collective continually threatens to dissolve the individual subject. In order to come to terms with their own memories of slavery, Sethe, Paul D, and Denver need to assign a limit to the work of mourning. In order to lead liveable lives they find it necessary to exorcise Beloved and the "more" of her infinite loss, to temporarily disremember the inconsolable lament of the dead. However, if exorcism turns out to be a necessary survival tactic for those who have only just made it across the Ohio, for Morrison and her contemporary readers "some kind of tomorrow" may be predicated on learning to live with ghosts, on acknowledging the presence of a past that cannot be fully reclaimed.

Each writer represents the past not as a continuous sequence of events leading up to the present, but as a form of mythic prehistory that constantly threatens to erupt into the present. My analysis has shadowed Freud's own scattered attempts to develop a psychoanalysis of culture that could account for the phenomenon of collective memory. In chapter 1, I briefly suggested a link between Coetzee's speculative allegories, which burrow beneath the ideological landscape of apartheid in order to expose the gaps in the story of South Africa that the ruling caste tells itself in order to justify its own existence, and Freud's attempts to excavate the prehistory of civilization in texts such as *Totem and Taboo* and *Moses and Monotheism*. In chapter 2, I showed how Harris's understanding of colonization as a precipitate collapse of time and memory is indebted to the Freudian understanding of trauma. And in chapter 3, I explored the link between Morrison's attempt to excavate the history of her race and Freud's attempts to reconstruct a prehistory of the Jews, showing how the Middle Passage, and to some extent slavery itself, constitutes a racial memory encrypted into the present time of the narrative.

It is possible to see the work of all three writers as ways of grappling with different forms of racial memory. Each attempts to relate a history of racial oppression that their readers are reluctant to confront. Coetzee gestures toward the story of oppression and torture that white South Africa would rather keep out of sight and mind. Harris insists on the history of colonization that contemporary Caribbean society would prefer not to dwell on. And Morrison returns to the history of slavery that the African American community finds itself unable to lay to rest. However, what gradually becomes clear is that these racial memories—these memories of racism—cannot be exclusively (re)claimed by any one section of the community. Disrupting the multicultural model of identity, racial memory functions as the common origin—and division—of the various "tribes" that make up contemporary society. To descend to the origin of racial difference is to lose sight of that difference, to recognize that the prehistory of one "tribe" is inextricably linked to that of others.

In *Moses and Monotheism*, Freud shows how the history of the Jewish tribe is bound up with the history of the Egyptians, from whom the Jews secretly inherited the monotheistic religion, and that of the Christians, to whom the Jews passed it on, along with the "memory" of having murdered the father. As I noted in my introduction, Caruth concludes her analysis of Freud's text by arguing that Freud's "central insight [is] that history, like trauma, is never simply one's own, that history is precisely the way in which we are implicated in one another's traumas" (192). This insight is most obviously applicable to Harris's work, which is specifically designed to debunk the myth of racial purity and to promote the idea of a cross-cultural inheritance that has its origins in the discontinuous history of colonization and slavery. However, it is also applicable to Coetzee's work, which might be described as the attempt to align the history of two traumas: that of the white South Africans who have heard and not heard the sounds coming from the granary and that of the black South Africans who have actually suffered the violence of apartheid. Similarly, the history of slavery is one that, as Morrison points out, neither black nor white people "want to remember." She describes *Beloved* as her attempt to disrupt what she refers to as a "*national* amnesia" (Angelo 257; emphasis added). And insofar as each of these novelists addresses their work beyond their national communities, one might say that the postcolonial work of mourning is designed to disrupt an *inter*national amnesia, the desire of both Europe and its ex-colonies to forget the histories of injustice that nevertheless determine present-day relations.

However, like Freud, the postcolonial novelist is engaged in a work of disruption rather than recovery, a revelation of the act of forgetting rather than of that which has been forgotten. Coetzee's speculative histories are unable to say for sure if Friday's home is the wreck of a slave ship. Harris is only able to effect a partial recovery of the fossilised history of the Caribbean. And Morrison places her "memories" of the Middle Passage within the disjointed consciousness of a ghost child who, like her sister, was never there. The inability to recover the prehistory of the tribe as an integrated and integratable narrative guarantees the endlessness of the process of collective mourning. To acknowledge an indeterminacy at the origin of the community is to celebrate what Ishmael lived out and Ahab died cursing, namely our "mortal inter-indebtedness" (Melville 482).[3]

NOTES

INTRODUCTION. SPECTERS OF COLONIALISM

1. Alternatively one could argue that apartheid and slavery are in fact exemplary forms of colonialism insofar as colonialism is predicated on the systematic denial of the humanity of the other. Such a definition of colonialism would differentiate between the experience of the settler and the experience of the colonized, or as Leela Gandhi puts it, "between histories of subjectivity and histories of subjection" (170). Australian and Canadian critics were among the first to locate their literary culture in postcolonial opposition to Empire—most famously in Ashcroft, Griffiths, and Tiffin's *The Empire Writes Back*. However, such a definition of the postcolonial risks repeating the racial "cover-up" behind the original construction of the Commonwealth. Robert Young argues that the Commonwealth was set up in the late nineteenth century to blur the distinction between the democratic Anglo-Saxon alliance of Britain and its white colonies and the despotic rule of subject races (38–39). In privileging racial oppression as the defining experience of colonialism, I do not wish to dismiss the importance of other aspects of colonialism but simply to explore the particular problems involved with memorializing racial oppression.

2. This performative conception of the postcolonial is echoed by Robert Young, who argues that "postcolonial theory is directed toward the active transformations of the present out of the clutches of the past" (4); by Peter Childs and Patrick Williams, who tentatively write "We could, however, argue for postcolonialism as an anticipatory discourse, recognizing that the condition which it names does not yet exist, but working nevertheless to bring it about" (7); and by Ato Quayson's understanding of postcolonialism as "a process of postcolonializing" (9). See also Sardar, Nandy, and Wyn Davies.

3. It is interesting to note the shift in Young's work. *White Mythologies* replicates the old polemic between Marxism and poststructuralism by repeatedly warning against the dangers of totalization. *Postcolonialism*, by contrast, while insisting on the importance of differential, context-specific analysis, places much more emphasis on the inspirational role of Marxism in anticolonial struggle and thus tacitly concedes the common concerns of Marxism and poststructuralism, something that I emphasize in chapter 1 by placing negative dialectics alongside deconstruction as similarly inconsolable projects.

4. Appiah argues that this appeal to an ethical universal is what distinguishes postcolonialism from postmodernism. Like the arguments of Tiffin and Adam, such an argument is harder to sustain in the wake of the ethicopolitical turn of writers such as Derrida.

5. At the level of biography—which Young perhaps makes too much of—it is important to remember that Derrida was born Jewish as well as Algerian.

6. See, for instance, Blanchot, Caruth, Lyotard, Hartman, Felman and Laub.

7. The systematic extermination of the Jews, as distinct from a policy of persecution and internment, did not begin until mid-1941.

8. "[What happens is that] our imagination strives to progress toward infinity, while our reason demands absolute totality as a real idea, and so [the imagination], our power of estimating the magnitude of things in the world of sense, is inadequate to that idea. Yet this inadequacy itself is the arousal in us of the feeling that we have within us a supersensible power . . ." (Kant 106, translator's brackets).

9. A more sustained reading of the causality of trauma in *The Satanic Verses* would have to take into account the implications of Rushdie's magical realist blend of comedy and tragedy and the way in which Gibreel and his double Chamcha function as each other's symptom.

10. My understanding of Benjamin is indebted to Annick Hillger's reading of *Fugitive Pieces* as a Benjaminian act of remembrance.

11. Interestingly, the French verb *conjurer* can mean both to conjure and to exorcise.

12. I am thinking of Siegfried Sassoon's famous poem "Aftermath" in which the commitment to remember the victims of the Great War is directed against the fear that it will all happen again: "Have you forgotten yet?/Look up and swear by the green of the spring that you'll never forget" (154).

13. My reference to Woolf's seminal novel may appear idiosyncratic to those who see modernist literature as embedded within a colonial tradition with which postcolonial literature makes an absolute break.

14. Walter Benjamin's analysis of the loss of proportion engendered by World War I is also relevant here. Benjamin argues that the modern novelist must bear witness to the "incommensurable" nature of modern experience ("The Storyteller" 87). Homi Bhabha's argument that this crisis of modernity must be understood from the perspective of the postcolonial would suggest that we see colonialism as engendering a similar crisis of storytelling. See, for instance, *The Location of Culture* 161, 175.

15. This is not to suggest that *Age of Iron* is an apolitical novel. It is, in fact, interesting precisely for the way in which it translates personal elegy into a mode of political protest.

16. This need to keep the question of what constitutes the human open is what powers the recent work of both Coetzee (*Disgrace* and *The Lives of Animals*) and Derrida ("The Animal That Therefore I Am [More to Follow]") on the distinction between the human and the animal.

17. See, for instance, Wole Soyinka's *Myth, Literature and the African World*.

18. See Maurice Blanchot's wonderful essay "Orpheus' Gaze."

19. Colonialism was the context for Althusser's "original" scene of interpolation; the subject who responds to a policeman's "hey you there!" is, according to Young, a colonial "subject regarded as already degraded" (*Postcolonialism* 417)

20. In Lacanian terms, that which is foreclosed from the Symbolic is destined to return in the Real. Fanon's psychoanalytic theorization of race has sparked a formidable critical industry. Homi Bhabha's poststructuralist "return" to Fanon in essays such as "Remembering Fanon: Self, Psyche and the Colonial Condition," published as the foreword to the 1985 edition of *Black Skin, White Masks,* has been usefully complicated by feminists such as Bergner (1995). The recent collection of essays edited by Christopher Lane and entitled *The Psychoanalysis of Race* (1999) continues to grapple with Fanon's legacy.

Chapter One. Speechless before Apartheid: J. M. Coetzee's Inconsolable Works of Mourning

1. For a deconstructive meditation on mourning and the TRC, see Dawes. For a useful set of essays on psychoanalysis and the TRC, see Moss and Sey.

2. See Krog 59–69 for an account of Dirk Coetzee's amnesty hearing.

3. Dante's tears are, as his guide points out, "impious," since they implicitly call into question God's judgment (Dante 20: 28–30). As such, they are perhaps the sign of what Dante himself was unable to articulate, the sign of his own nascent humanism.

4. While the end of apartheid has brought this day closer, it has become increasingly clear that full reconciliation is not possible without economic as well as political restitution. Coetzee's postapartheid fiction is thus in many respects gloomier than his early work. The theme of mourning also becomes more explicit in the later novels. *Age of Iron*, for instance, takes the form of a letter written by a mother dying of cancer to her estranged daughter, while *The Master of Petersburg* deals with Dostoevsky's grief at the death of his son. In his latest novel, *Disgrace*, a disgraced professor feels compelled to attend to the dying of unwanted dogs. Michael Marais's illuminating reading of Coetzee's work in the light of Blanchot's essay on "Orpheus' Gaze" tacitly confirms my emphasis on mourning insofar as Orpheus learns to use his lyre not to retrieve Eurydice but to turn his loss into art and his art into a work of inconsolable mourning.

5. See Vaughan and Knox-Shaw.

6. Ironically, *Lacanian Allegories* has been repeatedly criticized (Attwell "Problem" 594–97; Barnard 43–46) for its tendency to dehistoricize the novels, to reduce them, as the title suggests, to psychoanalytic parables.

7. It would require another chapter to determine whether Gordimer's novels truly constitute historical realism.

8. Jolly takes her idea of a frontier novel from Wilson Harris. In the next chapter I look at Harris's own frontier novels and their negotiation of the tension between the desire "to remain true to the violent domain of conquest in the present" and the need to suggest the "potential for transition."

9. Parry's critique of Coetzee's fiction is directed specifically against Attridge's championing of the deconstructive ethics of Coetzee's novels. As such, Parry's argument clearly parallels her critique of Spivak's "Can the Subaltern Speak?" in which Lyotard's concept of the *differend* is again pivotal.

10. Except for Susan Barton, the narrators do not have patronyms either. However, neither are they known exclusively by their first names. They are identified either by that ultimate linguistic sign of privilege, "I," or by their profession as magistrate or doctor.

11. Her blindness also prevents her from functioning as an eye-witness. The unwitnessable nature of torture is further emphasized by Colonel Joll's anachronistic sunglasses, which cause the Magistrate to wonder if he too is blind (1).

12. Felman and Laub's analysis of Holocaust testimony is relevant here. In her attempt to problematize the familiar notion of testimony, Felman analyzes testimonial texts that "do not simply report facts, but, in different ways, encounter—and make us encounter—strangeness" (7). I would argue that this encounter with strangeness is precisely the ethical destination of Coetzee's texts.

13. Derek Attridge has written extensively on the ethical dimension of Coetzee's work. My chapter builds on Attridge's work by relating interpersonal ethics to the ethics of historical relation and by linking both to a practice of inconsolable mourning.

14. For a fuller account of abjection, see the first chapter of Julia Kristeva's *Powers of Horror*. In *The Lives of Animals*, Coetzee's fictional doppelganger, Elizabeth Curren, seems to contradict the stalled trajectory of Coetzee's entire oeuvre in her declaration that "There are no bounds to the sympathetic imagination" (35). I explore this contradiction in "Becoming Stupid: The Limits of Empathy in J. M. Coetzee's *Disgrace*."

15. Lyotard's essay on "the jews" provides me with an exemplary alibi for my theoretical promiscuity, insofar as he also links the project of deconstruction to Adorno's comments on the possibility of art after Auschwitz (43–48) and to a certain psychoanalysis: "It follows that psychoanalysis, the search for lost time, can only be interminable, like literature and like true history (i.e., the one that is not historicism but anamnesis)" (20).

16. Menan du Plessis invokes the anti-idealist tradition of historical materialism in her excellent essay-review of *Waiting for the Barbarians*, "Towards a True Materialism" (1981). Her argument was largely ignored within South Africa, where critics persisted in describing Coetzee's work as "idealist" (Rich 388) or "metaphysical" (Martin 5).

17. Attwell ("J. M. Coetzee" 12) and Barnard (54) also cite Adorno's famous dictum. Neil Lazarus was the first to note the relevance of negative dialectics to Coet-

zee's work, in a 1986 article entitled "Modernism and Modernity: T. W. Adorno and Contemporary White South African Writing."

18. This is not to suggest that Foucault's work is naively historicist. *Madness and Civilization* in many ways anticipates Derrida's objections. Robert Young suggests that Foucault later took on board part of Derrida's critique and "substituted the idea of an otherness within reason for that of a repressed alterity existing outside or beyond it" (72).

19. De Man's work often seems to operate at a distance from political considerations. Derrida's *Mémoires* is partly motivated by a desire to show how de Man's version of deconstruction nevertheless involves a certain responsibility toward history.

20. "There is no document of civilization that is not at the same time a document of barbarity" (256).

21. Coetzee shortens Crusoe to Cruso and Defoe to Foe.

22. In *In the Heart of the Country,* Magda uses the term "speculative history" to refer to her attempt to construct the history of the "stone desert" in which she finds herself: "Then one day fences began to go up—I speculate of course—men on horseback rode up and from shadowed spaces issued invitations to stop and settle which might also have been orders . . ." (18). The tone is reminiscent of Freud's speculations on the prehistory of mankind, which, like Coetzee's novels, are often criticized for their refusal to provide a factual narrative. Both writers attempt not so much to recover the facts as to demonstrate the history of a Forgetting.

23. Other such moments would be the scenes of writing in which, left to his own devices at Foe's writing tablet or table, and equipped with a pen rather than a log, Friday (re)produces "walking eyes" (147) and "rows and rows of the letter *O*" (152).

24. Foe's reasoning is linked to Kristeva's notion of the "stranger within," developed in *Strangers Within Ourselves.*

25. See Eckstein for an excellent article on the inaccessibility of—and our responsibility toward—the other's pain in *Waiting for the Barbarians.*

26. Coetzee describes human relations under apartheid as "deformed and stunted" (*Doubling the Point* 98). Needless to say, many of the deformed relations of apartheid—inextricably linked as they are to the deformed relations of capitalism—linger on in postapartheid South Africa.

27. One of the targets of *Waiting for the Barbarians* is those South Africans who refuse(d) to acknowledge the systematic history of torture that underwrites their privilege. Faced with the testimony of torturers and their victims alike, Antjie Krog describes the ongoing refusal to admit to having heard the cries coming from the granary even while the TRC was in progress: "Whereas before people denied that atrocities happened, now they deny that they *knew* they were happening" (92).

28. My argument is partially indebted to a conference paper delivered by Rob Hughes, which also argued that the Magistrate is traumatized by the sounds coming from the granary.

29. In an interview, Coetzee says of Lacan that his "most inspired remarks have been about speaking from a position of doubt" (*Doubling* 29–30). In a lecture entitled "Of the Subject of Certainty," Lacan suggests that while both Descartes and Freud start out from a position of doubt, Descartes proceeds to banish doubt and move toward a position of certainty while Freud maintains a principle of doubt as his only certainty (Lacan 29–41).

30. The cover of the 1982 U.S. Penguin edition emphasizes the impossibility of this desire to make whole what has been smashed by depicting the Magistrate in the act of washing feet that have been literally severed from the barbarian girl's legs.

31. Of course, this "gift" is only a true gift to the extent that the Magistrate wills his own torture.

32. In "Becoming Stupid" I argue that stupidity, the circumvention of Reason, is in fact the ethical destination of Coetzee's fiction.

CHAPTER TWO. RITES OF COMMUNION: WILSON HARRIS'S HOSTING OF HISTORY

1. In an epigraph to the last book of *The Secret Ladder,* Harris quotes T. S. Eliot's famous lines from *The Four Quartets:* "A people without history/Is not redeemed from time, for history is a pattern/Of timeless moments" (*The Guyana Quartet* 445).

2. The Hebrew word *Shoah,* meaning simply destruction or annihilation, is often preferred.

3. Harris uses the term to describe the way in which Conrad's *Heart of Darkness* "stands upon a threshold of capacity to which Conrad pointed though he never attained that capacity himself" ("Frontier" 135)

4. Maes-Jelinek's critique of Coetzee parallels Harris's critique of the "consolidation of meaninglessness" that he sees in the work of other secular, post-Holocaust writers such as Camus and Robbe-Grillet ("Interior" 17).

5. Sharrad is aware of the contradiction without being able to account for it: "Harris revives the spirit of this forgotten technology [the *ars memoria*], applying it to those for whom Western technologies from the Renaissance on have meant oppression and oblivion" (119).

6. In "Literacy and the Imagination" Harris argues that "one may have to go further than the notion (the Nietzschean notion) that God is dead. It is not that God is dead, but that God may have ceased to be the kind of absolute author of events which one assumed him to be" (23). However, Nietzsche's affirmation of eternal return is precisely his own way of moving beyond the death of God. Harris's position here parallels his position on the death of the author. He wants to discard the notion of divine or authorial control, but retain the idea of a presiding spirit or witnessing presence.

7. Monumental history is the heroization of the nation's past, while antiquarian history is the museumification of the national heritage. Both these modes of history are forms of cultural memory, ways of memorializing the past in order to secure a collective identity in the present. In chapter 3, I suggest that Morrison's novels function *in part* as cultural memory, as a memorialization of African American identity. What in Nietzsche reads like a licensing-in-advance of the "Nazification" of history becomes in Morrison's work an important strategy of empowerment for an oppressed people. In both cases, memory operates as a mode of nationalism.

8. Recovering from long illness and depression, Nietzsche famously conceived of his philosophy as a "gay science": "'Gay Science': that signifies the saturnalia of a spirit who has patiently resisted a terrible, long pressure—patiently, severely, coldly, without submitting, but also without hope—and who is now all at once attacked by hope, the hope for health, and the intoxication of convalescence . . . a reawakened faith in a tomorrow and the day after tomorrow" (Preface to the Second Edition of *The Gay Science* 1). Harris may well have had this preface in mind in *Resurrection at Sorrow Hill*, in which Hope nurses Daemon out of his depression.

My conception of gay mourning is also intended to invoke Yeats's sense of how Hamlet and Lear are gay in the midst of tragedy, their "gaiety transfiguring all that dread" ("Lapis Lazuli" l.17). Written in 1938 the poem is all too aware of what Harris would describe as the coming storm. Like Benjamin's "Theses," written two years later, the poem attempts to achieve a view from above, a redemptive perspective on the catastrophe of history, ending with the vision of two Chinamen seated on the slopes of a mountain: "On all the tragic scene they stare./One asks for mournful melodies:/Accomplished fingers begin to play./Their eyes, mid many wrinkles, their eyes,/Their ancient glittering eyes, are gay" (ll. 51–55). Many thanks to Shirley Chew for drawing my attention to Yeats's poem.

9. An overwhelming majority of this work has been in relation to the Holocaust. See, for instance, Felman and Laub, Hartman, Caruth, Blanchot, Lyotard.

10. In a strange case of etymological miscegenation, the Pale also refers to the area of Russia to which Jews were confined.

Chapter Three. Keeping It in the Family: Passing on Racial Memory in the Novels of Toni Morrison

1. Trans. Clayton Eshleman and Annette Smith. The original reads: *"Mais qui tourne ma voix? qui écorche/ma voix? me fourrant dans la/gorge mille crocs de bambou"* (54).

2. My distinction in some ways parallels Saul Friedlander's distinction between a tractable "common memory" of the Holocaust and an intractable "deep memory" ("Trauma, Memory and Transference" 253).

3. See Shepherdson 44.

4. Whites may, however, be in possession of a different form of racial memory, insofar as the memory of having committed abuse may also provoke a form of collec-

tive, inherited trauma, as the comments by Morrison and Baldwin cited in the introduction would suggest. I suggest alternative forms of racial memory in the concluding chapter.

5. See Caruth 189.

6. This raises the difficult question of whether all experiences of racism are in some sense traumatic. While there is a clear difference between, say, an everyday experience of discrimination and Sethe's experience of having her breasts milked, I would argue that all experiences of racism contain the same traumatic kernel, insofar as even the so-called "casual" racial insult invokes a whole history of racial violation.

7. See, for example, Bennington and Young.

8. As I noted in the Introduction, Paul Gilroy speaks of a "slave sublime" in his reading of *Beloved* in *The Black Atlantic* (187–223). Sometimes referred to as simply "racial terror" the term would seem to derive from his reading of Burke and his analysis of Turner's painting of a slave ship (13–16) whereas Freeman's use of the sublime, in line with that of Lyotard and Žižek, derives from Kant's analysis of the sublime in *The Critique of Judgement.*

9. Wyatt also makes use of Spillers's complex historiography but fails to recognize the discrepancy between Spillers's creative yet faithful appropriation of Lacan's categories and her own contestation of them.

10. For further clarification of the difference between these natural and symbolic births and deaths, see Žižek (135), Durrant "How to Put his Story Next to Hers" (98–99), and Luckhurst (246).

11. Although critics such as Hirsch and Henderson associate Morrison's novelistic project with Sethe's rememory, Baby Suggs's approach to mourning and motherhood is clearly closer to Morrison's heart. In dedicating *Sula*, Morrison articulates her maternal love in a way that acknowledges the inevitability of loss: "It is sheer good fortune to miss somebody long before they leave you. This book is for Ford and Slade, whom I miss although they have not left me." Derrida also talks of a love that anticipates bereavement, a mourning that precedes the death of the loved one and accepts in advance the inevitability of loss. In "By Force of Mourning," dedicated to the memory of Louis Marin, he talks of "the undeniable anticipation of mourning that constitutes friendship" (188).

12. Eva's act of infanticide in *Sula* is motivated by precisely the opposite desire: she burns her son because she sees the state of dependency to which heroin has reduced him as an attempt to "get back up into my womb" (71).

13. Margaret Garner's surname may well have been that of her owner. Morrison gives the owner of Sweet Home and three of his slaves (the three Pauls) the same surname but we are never told Sethe's own surname. She would no doubt have adopted the name "Suggs," the surname of the man she claimed as her husband and of her mother-in-law.

14. This fantasy of a mother who "possesses the phallus" is structured in the same way as myths about the black man's potency; both fantasies cover over the symbolic castration, the lack of sociopolitical power, of ordinary mothers and black men.

15. Sethe's divergence from the Imaginary mother is at its sharpest here: where many theorists and practitioners of *écriture féminine* understand *jouissance* in terms of creative pleasure (Wyatt describes Denver's delight in written letters as a form of "verbal *jouissance*" [482]), *jouissance* in fact involves, as Slavoj Žižek has repeatedly argued, a destructive sadomasochistic enjoyment that moves it "beyond the pleasure principle."

16. The film version is particularly faithful to the novel in its refusal to explain these flashbacks: we are presented with images of the milking of Sethe's breasts and of Halle smearing butter over his face without being offered the connection between these events that Sethe offers us in the novel, namely that "the milk they took is on his mind" (70).

17. The essay was first delivered as a lecture at the University of Michigan in 1988, a year after the publication of *Beloved*. Part of this lecture is subsequently excerpted in afterwords to new editions, and part of it is developed in her critical study of race in American literature, *Playing in the Dark: Whiteness and the Literary Imagination*.

18. The complexity of Sethe's desire to lay it all down is increased by the pun on "lie": Sethe's actions both prove Baby Suggs a liar (89) and cause her to lie down.

Conclusion. Some Kind of Community

1. See Coetzee's *Disgrace* and *The Lives of Animals* and Derrida's "The Animal That Therefore I Am (More to Follow)."

2. The work of Derrida, Agamben, and Nancy on community is indebted to Maurice Blanchot's *The Unavowable Community* (1983).

3. Without venturing a reading of the complex racial dynamics of the novel, I would simply note that Ishmael owes his survival, and thus the telling of *Moby-Dick*, to his friendship with Queequeg, whose coffin, inscribed with the hieroglyphic marks of his own tattooed body, becomes Ishmael's "life-buoy" (583).

WORKS CITED

Achebe, Chinua. *Things Fall Apart*. 1959. New York: Ballantine, 1991.

Adam, Ian and Helen Tiffin. *Past the Last Post: Theorizing Post-Colonialism and Post-Modernism*. Hemel Hempstead: Harvester Wheatsheaf, 1991.

Adorno, Theodor. "Commitment." In *Aesthetics and Politics,* edited by Ronald Taylor. London: NLB, 1977.

Alighieri, Dante. *The Divine Comedy. Volume 1: Inferno.* Translated by Allen Mandelbaum. New York: Bantam, 1982.

Angelo, Bonnie. "The Pain of Being Black: An Interview with Toni Morrison." In *Conversations with Toni Morrison,* edited by Danielle Taylor-Guthrie. Jackson: University of Mississippi, 1994.

Agamben, Giorgio. *The Coming Community.* Translated by Michael Hardt. Minneapolis: University of Minnesota Press, 1993.

Attridge, Derek. "Oppressive Silence: J. M. Coetzee's *Foe* and the Politics of the Canon." In *Decolonizing Tradition: New Views of Twentieth Century 'British' Literary Canon,* edited by Karen Lawrence. Urbana: University of Illinois Press, 1992.

———. "Trusting the Other: Ethics and Politics in J. M. Coetzee's *Age of Iron*." *SAQ* 93.1 (1994): 59–81.

Attwell, David. *J. M. Coetzee: South Africa and the Politics of Writing*. Berkeley: University of California Press, 1993.

———. "J. M. Coetzee and South Africa: History, Narrative, and the Politics of Agency." PhD Dissertation, University of Texas at Austin, 1991.

———. "The Problem of History in the Fiction of J. M. Coetzee." *Poetics Today* 11 (1990): 579–615.

Barnard, Rita. "Dream Topographies: J. M. Coetzee and the South African Pastoral." *SAQ* 93.1 (1994): 33–58.

Begam, Richard. "Silence and Mut(e)ilation: White Writing in J. M. Coetzee's *Foe*." *SAQ* 93.1 (1994): 111–30.

Benjamin, Andrew. "The Crumbling Narrative: Time, Memory and Nihilism in *The Eye of the Scarecrow*." In *The Literate Imagination,* edited by Michael Gilkes. London: Macmillan, 1989.

Benjamin, Walter. "The Storyteller." *Illuminations,* translated by Harry Zohn. London: Cape, 1970.

————. "Theses on the Philosophy of History." *Illuminations,* translated by Harry Zohn. London: Cape, 1970.

Bennington, Geoffrey, and Robert Young, eds. *Poststructuralism and the Question of History.* Cambridge: Cambridge University Press, 1987.

Bergner, Gwen. "Who Is That Masked Woman? or The Role of Gender in Fanon's *Black Skin, White Masks.*" *PMLA* 110.1 (1995): 75–89.

Bhabha, Homi. *The Location of Culture.* London: Routledge, 1994.

————. "Representation and the Colonial Text: A Critical Exploration of Some Forms of Mimeticism." In *The Theory of Reading,* edited by Frank Gloversmith. Brighton: Harvester, 1984.

Blanchot, Maurice. "Orpheus' Gaze." 1955. In *The Siren's Song: Selected Essays of Maurice Blanchot,* edited by Gabriel Josipovici. Translated by Sacha Rabinovitch. Brighton: Harvester, 1982.

————. *The Unavowable Community.* 1983. Translated by Pierre Joris. Barrytown, N.Y.: Station Hill Press, 1988

————. *The Writing of the Disaster.* 1980. Translated by Ann Smock. Lincoln: University of Nebraska, 1995.

Brooks, Peter. *Reading for the Plot: Design and Intention in Narrative.* New York: Knopf, 1984.

Caruth, Cathy. "Unclaimed Experience: Trauma and the Possibility of Experience." In *Yale French Studies* 79, *Literature and the Ethical Question,* edited by Claire Novet. New Haven: Yale University Press, 1991.

Césaire, Aimé. "Notebook of a Return to the Native Land." *The Collected Works of Aimé Césaire,* translated by Clayton Eshleman and Annette Smith. Berkeley: University of California Press, 1983.

Childs, Peter, and Patrick Williams. *An Introductory Guide to Postcolonial Theory.* New York: Prentice Hall, 1997.

Coetzee, J. M. *Age of Iron.* Harmondsworth: Penguin, 1990.

————. *Disgrace.* London: Secker and Warburg, 1999

————. *Doubling the Point: Essays and Interviews.* Edited by David Attwell. Cambridge: Harvard University Press, 1992.

————. *Foe.* 1986. Harmondsworth: Penguin, 1987.

————. *In The Heart of the Country.* 1978. Harmondsworth: Penguin, 1982.

————. *Life and Times of Michael K.* 1983. Harmondsworth: Penguin, 1985.

————. *The Lives of Animals.* Edited by Amy Gutman. Princeton: Princeton University Press, 1999.

———. *The Master of Petersburg*. London: Martin, Secker and Warburg, 1994.

———. "The Novel Today." *Upstream* 6.1 (1988): 2–5.

———. *Waiting for the Barbarians*. 1980. Harmondsworth: Penguin, 1982.

———. *White Writing: On the Culture of Letters in South Africa*. New Haven and London: Yale University Press, 1988.

Copjec, Joan. *Read My Desire: Lacan Against the Historicists*. Cambridge: MIT University Press, 1994.

Darling, Marsha. "In the Realm of Responsibility: A Conversation with Toni Morrison." In *Conversations with Toni Morrison,* edited by Danielle Taylor-Guthrie. Jackson: University Press of Mississippi, 1994.

Dawes, Nicholas. "Constituting South Africa in the Fold of the 'Interim,' *Jouvert* 1.2 (1997). Jan 18th 1998 <http://social.chass.ncsu.edu/jouvert>.

Derrida, Jacques. "The Animal That Therefore I Am (More to Follow)." Translated by David Wills. *Critical Inquiry* 21.2 (2001): 369–418.

———. "By Force of Mourning." Translated by Pascale-Anne Brault, and Michael Naas. *Critical Inquiry* 22 (Winter 1996): 171–92.

———. "Cogito and the History of Madness. *Writing and Difference,* translated by Alan Bass. Chicago: University of Chicago Press, 1978.

———. "*Fors:* The Anglish *[sic]* Words of Nicolas Abraham and Maria Torok," Introduction to *The Wolf Man's Magic Word: A Cryptonomy,* by Nicolas Abraham and Maria Torok. Translated by Nicholas Rand. Minneapolis: Minnesota University Press, 1986.

———. *The Gift of Death*. Translated by David Wills. Chicago: University of Chicago Press, 1995.

———. *Mémoires for Paul de Man*. Translated by Eduardo Cadava, Jonathan Culler, Peggy Kamuf, and Cecile Lindsay. Edited by Cadava and Avita Ronell. New York: Columbia University Press, 1986.

———. *Specters of Marx: The State of the Debt, the Work of Mourning, and the New International*. Translated by Peggy Kamuf. New York and London: Routledge, 1994.

Defoe, Daniel. *Robinson Crusoe*. 1719. London: Signet, 1961.

———. *Roxana*. 1724. London: Oxford University Press, 1964.

Dovey, Teresa. *The Novels of J. M. Coetzee: Lacanian Allegories*. Johannesburg: Ad Donker, 1988.

Drake, Sandra. *Wilson Harris and the Modern Tradition: A New Architecture of the World*. Westport: Greenwood, 1986.

Du Plessis, Menan. "Towards a True Materialism." *Contrast* 13.4 (1981): 77–87.

Durrant, Samuel. "Bearing Witness to Apartheid: J. M. Coetzee's Inconsolable Works of Mourning." *Contemporary Literature* 40 (1999): 430–63.

——— . "Becoming Stupid: The Limits of Empathy in J. M. Coetzee's Work." *Alter-Nation* Special Edition 1, 2002 (forthcoming).

——— . "Coming Home 'Upon Threads of Desolation': The Reversal of Prophecy in Wilson Harris's *The Dark Jester*." In *Theatre of the Arts: Wilson Harris and the Caribbean,* edited by Hena Maes-Jelinek & Bénédicte Ledent. *Cross/Cultures* 60. Amsterdam/New York: Rodopi, 2002.

——— . "Hosting History: Wilson Harris's Sacramental Narratives." *Jouvert: An International Journal of Postcolonial Studies* 5.1 (2000), <http://social.chass.ncsu.edu/jouvert>.

——— . "How to Put His Story Next to Hers: Separating Subjects in Toni Morrison's *Beloved*." *Studies in Psychoanalytic Theory* 4.2 (1995): 96–112.

Eckstein, Barbara. "The Body, The Word and The State: J. M. Coetzee's *Waiting for the Barbarians*." *Novel* 22.2 (1989): 175–98.

Eliot, T. S. "The Four Quartets." *The Complete Poems and Plays*. London: Faber, 1969.

——— . "The Waste Land." *The Complete Poems and Plays*. London: Faber, 1969.

Fanon, Frantz. *Black Skin, White Masks*. 1952. Translated by Charles Lam Markmann. New York: Grove, 1967.

Felman, Shoshana, and Dori Laub. *Testimony: Crises of Witnessing in Literature, Psychoanalysis and History*. New York: Routledge, 1992.

Foucault, Michel. *Madness and Civilisation: A History of Insanity in the Age of Reason*. 1961. Translated by Richard Howard. New York: Vintage, 1988.

——— . "What Is an Author?" In *The Foucault Reader,* edited by Paul Rabinow. New York: Pantheon, 1984.

Freeman, Barbara. "Love's Labor: Kant, Isis and Toni Morrison's Sublime." *The Feminine Sublime*. Cambridge: Harvard University Press, 1995.

Freud, Sigmund. *Beyond the Pleasure Principle*. 1920. In *On Metapsychology*.

——— . "The Economic Problem of Masochism." In *On Metapsychology*.

——— . *Moses and Monotheism: Three Essays*. 1939. Vol. 23, *Standard Edition*.

——— . "Mourning and Melancholia." 1917. In *On Metapsychology*.

——— . *On Metapsychology: The Theory of Psychoanalysis*. Translated by James Strachey. Edited by Angela Richards. London: Penguin, 1991.

——— . "Remembering, Repeating and Working Through." 1914. Vol. 11, *Standard Edition*.

——— . *The Standard Edition of the Complete Works of Sigmund Freud*. Edited and translated by James Strachey. 24 vols. London: Hogarth, 1953–74.

Friedlander, Saul. "Trauma, Memory and Transference." In *Holocaust Remembrance: The Shapes of Memory,* edited by Geoffrey Hartman. Cambridge: Blackwell, 1995.

———, ed. *Probing the Limits of Representation: Nazism and the Final Solution*. Cambridge: Harvard University Press, 1992.

Gallagher, Susan Van Zanten. *A Story of South Africa: J. M. Coetzee's Fiction in Context*. Cambridge: Harvard University Press, 1991.

Gilkes, Michael, ed. *The Literate Imagination: Essays on Wilson Harris*. London: Macmillan, 1989.

———. *Wilson Harris and the Caribbean Novel*. Trinidad and Jamaica: Longman Caribbean, 1975.

Gilroy, Paul. *The Black Atlantic: Modernity and Double Consciousness*. London: Verso, 1993.

———. "Living Memory: A Meeting with Toni Morrison." *Small Acts: Thoughts on the Politics of Black Cultures*. London: Serpent's Tail, 1993.

Gordimer, Nadine. *Burger's Daughter*. 1979. London: Penguin, 1980.

———. "The Idea of Gardening." Review of *Life and Times of Michael K*. *New York Review of Books*, 2 February 1984: 3, 6.

———. *My Son's Story*. London: Penguin, 1991.

Handley, William. "The House a Ghost Built: Nommo, Allegory, and the Ethics of Reading in Toni Morrison's *Beloved*." *Contemporary Literature* 36 (1995): 676–701.

Harris, Wilson. "Adversarial Contexts and Creativity." *New Left Review* 154.6 (1985): 124–28.

———. *Carnival. The Carnival Trilogy*. London: Faber, 1993.

———. *Explorations: A Selection of Talks and Articles*. Edited by Hena Maes-Jelinek. Mundelstrup, Denmark: Dangaroo Press, 1981.

———. "The Frontier on Which *Heart of Darkness* Stands." In *Explorations*.

———. *The Guyana Quartet*. London: Faber and Faber, 1985.

———. "History, Fable and Myth in the Caribbean and the Guianas." In *Explorations*.

———. "Interior of the Novel: Amerindian/African/European Relations." In *Explorations*.

———. "Literacy and the Imagination." In *The Literate Imagination: Essays on Wilson Harris*, edited by Michael Gilkes. London: Macmillan, 1989.

———. "A Note on the Genesis of *The Guyana Quartet*." *The Guyana Quartet*. London: Faber, 1985.

———. *Resurrection at Sorrow Hill*. London: Faber and Faber, 1993.

———. "A Talk on the Subjective Imagination." In *Explorations*.

———. "Tradition and the West Indian Novel." *Tradition, the Writer and Society*. London, New Beacon, 1987.

Hartman, Geoffrey. "The Book of the Destruction." In *Probing the Limits of Representation: Nazism and the Final Solution,* edited by Saul Friedlander. Cambridge: Harvard University Press, 1995.

———, ed. *Holocaust Remembrance: The Shapes of Memory.* Cambridge: Blackwell, 1994.

Hegel, G. W. F. *Lectures on the Philosophy of World History.* 1822–27. Translated by H. B. Nisbet. Introduction by Duncan Forbes. Cambridge: Cambridge University Press, 1975.

Henderson, Mae G. "Toni Morrison's *Beloved:* Re-Membering the Body as Historical Text." In *Comparative American Identities: Race, Sex and Nationality in the Modern Text. Essays from the English Institute,* edited by Hortense Spillers. New York: Routledge, 1991.

Hillger, Annick. "'Afterbirth of Earth': Messianic Materialism in Anne Michaels's *Fugitive Pieces." Canadian Literature* 160 (Spring 1999): 28–45.

Hirsch, Marianne. "Maternity and Rememory: Toni Morrison's *Beloved."* In *Representations of Motherhood,* edited by Donna Bassin et al. New Haven: Yale University Press, 1994.

Hughes, Rob. "Reading Trauma and *Nachträglichkeit* in the Post-Colonial Text." Paper delivered at the Association for the Psychoanalysis of Culture and Society Conference on "Psychoanalysis and Postcolonialism," George Washington University, 13 October 13 1995. Unpublished.

Jolly, Rosemary Jane. "Territorial Metaphor in Coetzee's *Waiting for the Barbarians." Ariel* 20.2 (1989): 69–79.

Kant, Immanuel. *Critique of Judgement.* 1790. Translated by Werner S. Pluhar. Indiana: Hackett, 1987

Knox-Shaw, Peter. "*Dusklands:* A Metaphysics of Violence." *Contrast* 14 (1982): 26–38.

Kristeva, Julia. *Powers of Horror: An Essay on Abjection.* Translated byLeon S. Roudiez. New York: Columbia University Press, 1982.

———. *Strangers to Ourselves.* Translated by Leon S. Roudiez. New York: Columbia University Press, 1991.

Lacan, Jacques. *Écrits: A Selection.* 1966. Translated by Alan Sheridan. London and New York: Routledge, 1995.

———. "Of the Subject of Certainty." 1973. In *The Four Fundamental Concepts of Psychoanalysis,* edited by Jacques-Alain Miller. Translated by Alan Sheridan. London: Penguin, 1994.

Lane, Christopher, ed. *The Psychoanalysis of Race.* New York: Columbia University Press, 1998.

Laub, Dori. "An Event Without a Witness: Truth, Testimony and Survival." In *Testimony: Crises of Witnetssing in Literature,* edited by Shoshana Felman, and Dori Laub. New York: Routledge, 1992.

Lazarus, Neil. "Modernism and Modernity: T. W. Adorno and Contemporary White South African Writing." *Cultural Critique* 5 (1986): 131–55.

Lyotard, Jean-François. *Heidegger and "the jews."* Minneapolis: University of Minnesota Press, 1990.

Luckhurst, Neil. "Impossible Mourning in Toni Morrison's *Beloved* and Michèle Roberts's *Daughters of the House.*" *Critique: Studies in Contemporary Fiction* 37 (1996): 243–60.

Maes-Jelinek, Hena. "Ambivalent Clio: J. M. Coetzee's *In The Heart of the Country* and Wilson Harris's *Carnival.*" *Journal of Commonwealth Literature* 22.1 (1987): 87–98.

Marais, Michael. "'Little enough, less than little: nothing': Ethics, Engagement, and Change in the Fiction of J. M. Coetzee." *Modern Fiction Studies* 46.1 (2000): 159–82.

Martin, Paul. "Narrative, History, Ideology: A Study of *Waiting for the Barbarians* and *Burger's Daughter.*" *Ariel* 17.3 (1986): 3–21.

Marx, Karl. "The Eighteenth Brumaire of Louis Bonaparte." 1852. In *The Marx-Engels Reader,* edited by Robert C. Tucker. New York: Norton, 1978.

Matus, Jill. *Toni Morrison. Contemporary World Writers.* Manchester: Manchester University Press, 1998.

McKay, Nellie. "An Interview with Toni Morrison." In *Conversations with Toni Morrison,* edited by Danielle Taylor-Guthrie. Jackson: University of Mississippi Press, 1994.

Melville, Herman. *Moby-Dick.* Edited by Tony Tanner. Oxford: Oxford University Press, 1988.

Michaels, Anne. *Fugitive Pieces.* Toronto: McClleland and Stuart, 1996.

Montrélay, Michèle. "The Story Of Louise." In *Returning to Freud: Clinical Psychoanalysis in the School Of Lacan,* edited by Stuart Schneiderman. New Haven: Yale University Press, 1980.

Morrison, Toni. *Beloved.* 1987. London: Picador, 1988.

———. *Jazz.* 1992. London: Penguin, 1993.

———. *Paradise.* New York: Knopf, 1998.

———. *Playing in the Dark: Whiteness and the Literary Imagination.* London: Picador, 1993.

———. *Sula.* 1974. London: Picador, 1991.

———. *Song of Solomon.* 1977. New York: Knopf, 1978.

———. *Tar Baby.* 1981. London: Picador, 1991.

———. *The Bluest Eye.* 1970. London: Penguin, 1994.

———. "The Site of Memory." In *Inventing the Truth: The Art and Craft of Memoir,* edited by William Zinsser. Boston: Houghton Mifflin, 1987.

————. "Unspeakable Things Unspoken: the African-American Presence in American Literature." The Tanner Lecture on Human Values, University of Michigan, 7 October 1988. *Michigan Quarterly Review* 28 (1989): 1–34.

Moses, Michael Valdez. "Solitary Walkers: Rousseau and Coetzee's *Life and Times of Michael K.*" *SAQ* 93.1 (1994): 131–57.

Moss, Donald, and James Sey, eds. *South Africa*. Special Issue of *American Imago* 55.1 (1998).

Moyers, Bill. "A Conversation with Toni Morrison." In *Conversations with Tony Morrison*, edited by Danielle Taylor-Guthrie. Jackson: University of Mississippi Press, 1994.

Nancy, Jean-Luc. *The Inoperative Community*. 1985–6. Edited by Peter Connor. Translated by Peter Connor and Lisa Garbus. Minneapolis: University of Minnesota Press, 1991.

Nietzsche, Friedrich. 1872. *The Birth of Tragedy and the Genealogy of Morals*. Translated by Francis Golffing. New York: Doubleday, 1990.

————. "On the Uses and Disadvantages of History for Life." 1873. *Untimely Meditations*. Edited by Daniel Breazeale. Translated by R. J. Hollingdale. Cambridge: Cambridge University Press, 1997.

Parry, Benita. "Speech and Silence in the Fictions of J. M. Coetzee." In *Critical Perspectives on J. M. Coetzee*, edited by Graham Huggan and Stephen Watson. London: Macmillan, 1996.

Peach, Linden, ed. *Toni Morrison: Contemporary Critical Essays*. New Casebooks. New York: St. Martin's Press, 1998.

Penner, Dick. "Sight, Blindness and Double Thought in J. M. Coetzee's *Waiting for the Barbarians*." *World Literature Written in English* 26.1 (1986): 34–45.

Poynting, Jeremy. "Half Dialectical, Half Metaphysical: 'The Far Journey of Oudin.'" In *The Literate Imagination: Essays on Wilson Harris*, edited by Michael Gilkes. London: Macmillan, 1989.

Quayson, Ato. *Postcolonialism: Theory, Practice or Process?* Cambridge, Eng.: Polity, 2000.

Rich, Paul. "Apartheid and the Decline of the Civilisation Idea: An Essay on Nadine Gordimer's *July's People* and J. M. Coetzee's *Waiting for the Barbarians*." *Research in African Literatures* 15 (1984): 365–93.

Ruas, Charles. "Toni Morrison." In *Conversations with Tony Morrison*, edited by Danielle Taylor-Guthrie. Jackson: University of Mississippi Press, 1994.

Sardar, Zia, Ashis Nandy, and Merryl Wyn Davies. *Barbaric Others: A Manifesto on Western Racism*. London: Pluto Press, 1993.

Sassoon, Siegfried. "Aftermath." In *Up the Line to Death: The War Poets 1914–18*, edited by Brian Gardner. London: Methuen, 1964.

Scarry, Elaine. *The Body in Pain: The Making and Unmaking of the Self*. Oxford: Oxford University Press, 1985

Seshadri-Crooks, Kalpana. "The Comedy of Domination: Psychoanalysis and the Conceit of Whiteness." In *The Psychoanalysis of Race,* edited by Christopher Lane. New York: Columbia University Press, 1998.

Shakespeare, William. *Hamlet.* 1601. *The Complete Works of William Shakespeare.* Edited by Peter Alexander. London: Diamond, 1994.

Sharrad, Paul. "The Art of Memory and the Liberation of History: Wilson Harris's Witnessing of Time." *Journal of Commonwealth Literature* 27.1 (1992): 110–27.

Shaw, Gregory. "The Novelist as Shaman." In *The Literate Imagination: Essays on Wilson Harris,* edited by Michael Gilkes. London: Macmillan, 1989.

Shepherdson, Charles. "Human Diversity and the Sexual Relation." In *The Psychoanalysis of Race,* edited by Christopher Lane. New York: Columbia University Press, 1998.

Spillers, Hortense. "Mama's Baby, Papa's Maybe: An American Grammar Book." *Diacritics* 17 (1987): 65–81.

Spivak, Gayatri Chakravorty. "Can the Subaltern Speak?" In *Marxism and the Interpretation of Culture,* edited by Cary Nelson and Lawrence Grossberg. London: Macmillan, 1988.

———. *A Critique of Postcolonial Reason: Toward a History of the Vanishing Present.* Cambridge: Harvard University Press, 1999.

———. "Theory in the Margin: Coetzee's *Foe* Reading Defoe's *Crusoe/Roxana.*" In *Consequences of Theory,* edited by Jonathan Arac and Barbara Johnson. Baltimore: Johns Hopkins University Press, 1991.

Stambaugh, Joan. *Nietzsche's Thought of Eternal Return.* Baltimore: Johns Hopkins University Press, 1972.

Taylor-Guthrie, Danille, ed. *Conversations with Toni Morrison.* Jackson: University Press of Mississippi, 1994.

Vaughan, Michael. "Literature and Politics: Currents in South African Writing in the Seventies." *Journal of South African Studies* 9.1 (1982): 18–38.

Woolf, Virginia. *Mrs Dalloway.* 1925. San Diego: Harcourt, Brace, 1990.

Wyatt, Jean. "Giving Body to the Word: The Maternal Symbolic in Toni Morrison's *Beloved.*" *PMLA* 108.3 (1993): 474–88.

Yates, Frances. *The Art of Memory.* London: Routledge, Kegan Paul, 1966.

Yeats, William Butler. "Lapis Lazuli." 1892. In *The Norton Anthology of English Literature,* edited by Abrams et al. Sixth ed. Vol. 2. New York: Norton, 1993.

Young, Robert. *Postcolonialism: An Historical Introduction.* Oxford: Blackwell, 2001.

———. *White Mythologies: Writing History and the West.* London and New York: Routledge, 1990.

Žižek, Slavoj. *The Sublime Object of Ideology.* London: Verso, 1989.

INDEX

Robinson Crusoe, 32, 34, 37
Rushdie, Salman, 5, 7, 120

Sassoon, Siegfried, 120
Scarry, Elaine, 16
Secret Ladder, The (Harris), 56, 124
Sekyi-Otu, Ato, 15, 21
Senghor, Léopold, 15
Sharrad, Paul, 62, 124
Shaw, Gregory, 60, 61, 121
Shepherdson, Charles, 112, 125
slavery, 2, 4, 5, 7, 19–21, 34, 63, 64, 68,
    81, 83, 88, 89, 92–99, 102, 113, 115,
    116, 119
Song of Solomon (Morrison), 82, 86
South Africa, 14, 17, 18, 23–26, 29, 38,
    42, 58, 59, 123
Specters of Marx (Derrida), 1, 2, 13, 60,
    64, 66, 72
Spillers, Hortense, 87, 88, 89, 94, 97,
    126
Spivak, Gayatri Chakravorty, 7, 8, 12,
    16, 17, 112, 122
subaltern, 6, 7, 16, 17, 39
sublime, 3, 4, 5, 17, 63, 86, 93, 126

Tar Baby (Morrison), 82
terra nullius, 17
testimony, 23, 26, 55, 122, 123
The Bluest Eye (Morrison), 82, 100, 101

The Lives of Animals (Coetzee), 120,
    122, 127
The Waste Land (T. S. Eliot), 55, 63, 73
Torok, Maria, 31
torture, 42, 43, 44, 46, 47, 48, 116, 122,
    123, 124
trauma, 3–10, 14, 16, 19, 40, 45, 63, 68,
    69, 82–89, 93, 98, 109, 116, 120,
    126
    individual vs. collective, 4, 11, 14, 21,
    54, 63, 64, 84
Truth and Reconciliation Commission
    (TRC), 23, 24, 51, 121, 123

Waiting for the Barbarians (Coetzee), 25,
    26, 32, 36, 41, 42, 49, 50, 57, 66, 114,
    122, 123
Whole Armour, The (Harris), 56
Woolf, Virginia, 10, 120
working through, 10, 11, 23, 24, 28, 44,
    45, 46, 50, 63, 79, 83, 101
Wyatt, Jean, 87, 88, 90, 91, 92, 93, 94,
    95, 97, 102, 108, 126, 127

Yeats, William, 125
Yoruba, 13
Young, Robert, 2, 3, 119, 120, 121, 123,
    126

Žižek, Slavoj, 90, 126, 127